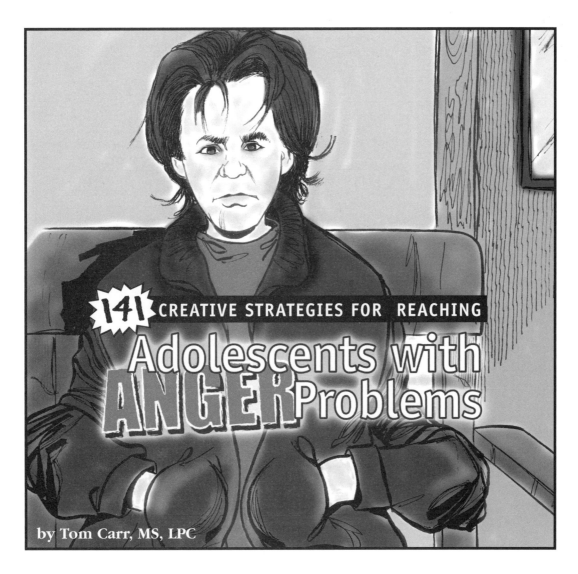

141 CREATIVE STRATEGIES FOR REACHING
Adolescents with ANGER Problems

by Tom Carr, MS, LPC

youth light
inc.

© 2007, 2005 by YouthLight, Inc.
Chapin, SC 29036

Design and Layout by Diane Florence • Project Editing by Susan Bowman

ISBN
1-889636-86-X

Library of Congress Number
2005920810

10 9 8 7 6 5 4 3 2
Printed in the United States

Table of Contents

Table of Contents
(continued)

Acknowledgements

Thanks to Aaron Carr, my son and fellow educator, for helping me put this book together.

Thank you to Jamie Allison, for her article on the benefits of yoga for adolescents.

Dedications

I dedicate this book to those professionals who devote so much of their time and energy working with today's challenging adolescents.

Introduction

In 2000 I wrote a very successful selling book on children with anger problems. In the summer of 2004 I began the task of writing another book on anger. This time the focus was on adolescents. While doing my research I was surprised to find that there were very few practical books out there for helping teachers and parents with their angry adolescents. Most of the books I did find seem to have a common format. The books were usually 150 pages long with 130 pages centered on the causes and affects of anger, leaving only a few pages for strategies. I wanted to write a book with the opposite format, one that had only a few pages of theory, causes and affects, and, which contained numerous pages of creative tools for teachers and parents. This book does provide the reader with some of the common causes of anger in our young people, but the bulk of the book is filled with 141 strategies that are divided in to five categories (levels of anger). Included are over twenty-five reproducible skill sheets to assist teachers, parents, and students.

As I began the process of putting this book together, the southeastern part of the United States was pounded by several powerful hurricanes. Throughout the summer I witnessed news stories about the damages done by Charley, Frances, Ivan, and Jeanne. The more I watched the television reports and read the newspapers, the more I realized that there were many comparisons between hurricanes and the stages of anger in adolescents. I eventually decided to write this book using the analogy of, "the stages of anger in young people are comparable to the categories of severity of hurricanes."

How are hurricanes and angry adolescents alike? Let's take a look.

- If you live in the Southeast, especially along the Atlantic Coast, hurricanes are inevitable. If you parent or teach adolescents, inevitably they will go through stages of anger.

- Hurricanes are categorized into levels of severity. Small, less powerful storms are a Category 1 or 2 while the more destructive ones reach a Category 4 or 5. Adolescents also travel through stages and categories. Some display low levels of anger while a small number reach a Category 5 and become dangerous and destructive.

- Just as hurricanes pass through and leave, we also find that the turbulent period of adolescent anger will pass. We must be patient and realize that most of us adults went through a rebellious period in our lives.

- Thanks to modern technology, we are given many warnings about hurricanes heading our way. If we closely observe children, we'll notice warning signs that tell us of impending trouble.

- We can prepare for a hurricane, but we can't stop it from hitting. Home owners can board up windows, gather up lawn furniture, stock shelves with extra food, buy batteries, purchase generators, and seek shelter in their basements, but the storm will arrive. Being preventive in nature will help lessen the effects of the storm. Parents and teachers can do many preventive interventions with adolescents, but their angry periods will arrive. Hopefully the preventive strategies will lessen the severity of their anger.

- There are many things "not to do" when the hurricane hits (i.e. don't go outside, don't be near windows, don't leave your pets outside, etc). There are also many things "not to do" when a student gets angry. There are many things that parents and teachers can do to make things worse.

- Some hurricanes may be so dangerous that families have to leave their homes and move inland until they pass. In extreme cases, an adolescent may have to

Introduction

temporarily "move inland." He or she might be removed from the home or school for a period of time to get extra help.

■ After the storm passes, home owners assess the damage, make repairs, and prepare for the next one. Teachers and parents need to follow the same guidelines as home owners. After an outburst, adults need to assess the damage, repair/restore relationships, encourage forgiveness and apologies, make the child responsible for his/her action, and discuss ways of preventing problems in the future. Ask the question, "What did I learn from this latest anger episode?"

I've divided this book in to five categories based on severity and taken the rating scale used with hurricanes and adjusted it in a way that helps adults recognize levels of anger in children. Each of the five categories has strategies applicable to that level. For instance, Category 1 contains mostly preventive measures while Category 4 contains strategies to use when a student is in the process of venting anger in an inappropriate manner.

HURRICANES

Category	Wind Speed	Description
1	74-95	mild
2	96-110	moderate
3	111-130	strong
4	131-155	very strong
5	156 and up	devastating

ANGER

Category	Description	Types of Strategies Presented
1	mild	mostly preventive
2	moderate	preventive, quick, easy to use
3	strong	fairly strong, firm interventions
4	very strong	safety issues, seeking assistance
5	devastating	safety issues, possible removal from class, school, home. Long term interventions.

I have also included another, more-detailed rating scale (see Strategy #1) called the Beaufort Wind & Student Anger Scale. This unique scale compares wind speed with thirteen different levels of anger. Teachers will find this rating tool very helpful when discussing student behaviors with counselors, psychologists, principals, and parents.

Anyone who works with adolescents must realize that there are no "quick fixes" when it comes to anger problems. This book provides readers with over a hundred strategies that can be successful with most young people. Unfortunately these interventions do not work with some of the more extreme cases. Outside professional help may be needed. Teachers may need to make referrals for testing and/or counseling. Finally, a very small number of these adolescents may need to be removed and institutionalized for a period of time before returning to home or school. Don't give up on these difficult, combative, defiant, and dangerous students! With our help, compassion, patience, and assistance, most adolescents can "weather the storm" and be successful.

Introduction
(continued)

POSSIBLE CAUSES OF ANGER IN ADOLESCENTS

There are numerous causes of anger and they may vary based on age level. For instance, what causes a young child to get angry doesn't bother an adult. The things that upset an adult may be of no concern to a thirteen-year-old. In my first book on anger, *131 Creative Strategies for Reaching Children with Anger Problems*, I presented many causes of anger in young children. Below are several possible causes of anger specifically aimed at adolescents.

- **Having only one parent.** According to the U.S. Census Bureau, 28% of all children in the U.S. under 18 live with only one parent. The single parent has little support in raising difficult children. Statistics often reveal that most gang members have no fathers in the house so they turn to the streets to get some of their basic needs met.

- **Having parents that are "too strict."** Children raised in authoritarian households seldom have much freedom, are not allowed to question or challenge authority, or are allowed to seek independence. These children are raised by fear of punishment. Anger builds in these children and they often have outbursts and meltdowns in places other than the home. Authoritarian parents do not allow their children to express anger in the home.

- **Having permissive-indulgent parents.** These parents are always providing too many "nets" for their children. They are always there to catch their children when they fall. They never let their children experience uncomfortable consequences. They give their children whatever they want and seldom say "no." Eventually there comes a time when mom and dad can't help them and they become "spoiled" and angrier at the world.

- **Learning problems.** Many children with learning problems can navigate their way through elementary school, but when they get to middle school, things change for the worse. Students with learning disabilities, attention problems, and those who are slow learners often get frustrated and develop anger problems.

- **Learning and teaching style differences.** I am aware of numerous cases of students who do well in one teacher's classroom and who are behavior problems in another. Often the problems occur when there are miss-matches in teaching and learning styles.

- **Moody, irritable temperaments.** Some people are born with a difficult temperament. They have no disorders; they are just a bit more moody and irritable than others.

- **Inflated self-esteems.** In the June 12, 2003 issue of *Web MD Health*, Michael Smith reports on a study that shows that the self-esteems of college students are at a twenty year high. He offers the thought, "But are things getting any better in reference to drug use, violence, teen pregnancy, etc.?" Are we guilty of over doing it with self-esteem inflation? Do we praise too much and give out too many stickers and gold stars? Do we reward students with undeserved certificates, medals, and trophies? Are we afraid to let a child fail? Students with inflated self-esteems often get angry when they enter the real world where they do not always receive a pat on the back for a job well done.

- **They are overly active.** Some adolescents get involved in too many activities and eventually they get "burnt out." They self-created such a hectic schedule that they seldom have time to relax and unwind.

Introduction

■ **Peer issues.** Every student has to deal with bullying, teasing, and getting along with others. Any teacher in middle school will tell you that peer issues cause numerous anger problems and classroom disruptions.

■ **Academic competition.** A small number of students get so focused on getting high grades that they get angry when they don't get an "A." Many become perfectionists.

■ **They are not outdoors enough.** There is a Native American proverb that states, "The more we remove ourselves from the land, the worse our behaviors gets." Children are spending way too much time inside watching television, playing video games, and looking at computer screens. They need to be outside to get some sun, to appreciate nature, to exercise, and to interact with friends.

■ **Drug and alcohol use.** Many adolescents experiment with drugs and alcohol which can cause changes in behavior.

■ **Living in troubled neighborhoods.** Some children have to develop a tough, angry personality just to survive in their neighborhood.

■ **Viewing too much violence.** Many are spending a great deal of their free time watching violent movies and playing violent video games. This can cause adolescents to become more aggressive and express less empathy toward others.

■ **Not enough sleep.** Our children are not getting enough sleep. We know how a lack of sleep can affect behavior.

■ **Family issues.** Children living in homes riddled with abuse, alcohol, and violence pay the price when they enter school. Children living in poverty also feel pain.

■ **Lack of nurturing.** Adolescents still need love, hugs, affection, and a daily, "I love you" at home.

■ **Exposure to trauma.** Children who have experienced and/or witnessed extreme traumas often are prone to anger episodes.

■ **Families are too mobile.** In today's society, many families are on the move. Many children end up attending several different schools before they graduate and this makes it difficult for them to develop lasting relationships. Also, because of our mobile society, children are no longer closely involved with grand-parents and other relatives who could help provide love and guidance.

■ **Anger associated with disorders.** Teachers and parents must do their homework and learn all they can about the disorders of their children. Students with Oppositional Defiant Disorder, Conduct Disorder, Bi-polar Disorder, ADHD, and Asperger's are going to have more anger issues than others in class.

Here are a few final thoughts before reading on. I encourage readers to always start at the beginning of the book. Use the preventive measures in Category 1 as much as possible. Hopefully this may prevent having to use some of the Category 4 and 5 strategies. Believe it or not, there will be times when you are dealing with a very difficult situation and you'll find that a lower level intervention (Category 1 or 2) may be more effective than a Category 4 or 5. Also, one of our goals is to help students begin to monitor and control their anger. Utilize the many skill sheets and activities on a regular basis in your classroom as a preventive measure. Included are a few skill sheets for parents. Teachers, make sure you pass them on.

CATEGORY 1:
MILD ANGER

Strategy #1

A UNIQUE ANGER SCALE

In 1806, Sir Francis Beaufort created the Beaufort Wind Scale to help sailors as they ventured out to sea. His scale was based on observations. By studying such things as smoke rising from chimneys, leaves falling from trees, branches breaking off limbs, and spinning vanes, sailors could estimate wind speed. I was fascinated by the cleverness of his scale and decided to adjust it to help teachers estimate anger levels from classroom observations. Most anger scales are rather vague and have a rating of 1-10. My Beaufort Wind & Student Anger Scale gives observers **thirteen** ratings (0-12) and it provides a more in depth description of the characteristics and mannerisms of angry students.

Teachers, counselors, and parents can utilize this unique scale on a daily basis when communicating with each other. Here are a few examples.

- Jenny's mother calls the teacher on a daily basis to monitor her daughter's anger levels.

- When the music teacher senses Brandon is getting upset and may need to leave the room, she can call the counselor and give a rating on the scale on how angry he is. Then the counselor can make a decision to go to the music room immediately or to wait a while.

- Teachers can monitor a student in different settings. Does he have a higher rating in the classroom or on the playground?

- Teachers can rate Chip on a daily basis in order to see if his anger is getting better or worse.

- The scale can be used in a way that shows respect for the student. Instead of talking on the phone to the principal in front of the class and saying, "Sidney is throwing things and pounding her fists on her desk," all the teacher has to say is, "She's at #9."

Make copies of Skill Sheet #1 and give one to everybody on the staff who deals with challenging students. This rating scale can eliminate a lot of unnecessary conversations between teachers, principals, counselors, social workers, psychologists, and parents.

BEAUFORT WIND & STUDENT ANGER SCALE

WIND: MILES PER HOUR, OBSERVATIONS	SCALE	ANGER: LEVEL, BEHAVIORS, OBSERVATIONS
Calm: Less than 1mph. Calm, smoke rises vertically.	0	Student is calm, humming, smiling, patient, very cooperative, getting along well with others.
Light air: 1-3mph. Direction of wind shown by smoke but not by wind vanes.	1	A bit quiet, cooperative, still interacting well with teacher and classmates.
Light breeze: 4-7mph. Wind felt on face, leaves rustle; vanes moved by wind.	2	An occasional frown, tiny bit irritable, a little slow to cooperate with teacher and/or peers.
Gentle breeze: 8-12mph. Leaves and small twigs in constant motion; wind extends light flag.	3	Increase in irritability, keeping more to self, restless, attention and focus problems.
Moderate breeze: 13-18mph. Raises dust and loose paper; small branches are moved.	4	Mumbling, complaining, wants to be left alone, restless, more frowning, struggles to cooperate.
Fresh breeze: 19-24mph. Small leaves in trees begin to sway; crested wavelets form on inland waters,	5	Verbalizes his anger, "Leave me alone!" Squeezes fist, starts to shut down, sweating, flushness in face.
Strong breeze: 25-31mph. Large branches in motion; telegraph wires whistle; umbrellas used with difficulty.	6	Trouble sitting still, more complaining, very slow to cooperate, glares at others, calls other students "dumb" or "stupid."
Moderate gale: 32-38mph. Whole trees in motion; inconvenience in walking against the wind.	7	Begins to backtalk, disrespectful, rolls eyes at teacher, goes "face to face" with peers. Makes a fist or picks up something and pretends to throw.
Fresh gale: 39-46mph. Breaks twigs off trees; generally impedes progress.	8	Begins a meltdown, pounds fists on desk, hits wall, throws things on floor, disrupts class.
Strong gale: 47-54mph. Slight structural damage occurs; chimney pots and slates removed.	9	Appears ready to explode, threatens to hurt self or others, will not follow teacher's orders, says, "You can't make me," or "I don't care."
Whole gale: 55-63mph. Trees uprooted; considerable structural damage occurs.	10	Puts hands on others, pushes, shoves. Starts to hurt self, breaks and/or throws things.
Storm: 64-72mph. Very rarely experienced; accompanied by widespread damage.	11	Starts to hit/hurt others, seldom throws more than one or two punches. Teacher can pull him away.
Hurricane: 73+mph. Devastation occurs.	12	In a rage, totally out of control, will not stop hitting or stop throwing things, destroys room, takes more than one adult to restrain him.

Adapted from the Beaufort Wind Scale developed by Admiral Sir Francis Beaufort in 1806.

Strategy #2

AVOID THE 7 DEADLY HABITS

In his book, *Unhappy Teenagers*, Dr. William Glasser lists what he calls, "The Seven Deadly Habits" which many adults employ in an effort to "change" an adolescent's negative behavior. The seven habits are listed below. Glasser notes that almost all relationships can be saved by giving up the deadly habits. When dealing with a difficult, angry adolescent, the worse habit to use is criticism. Criticism does nothing but add fuel to the fire.

THE SEVEN DEADLY HABITS

- Criticizing
- Blaming
- Complaining
- Nagging
- Threatening
- Punishing
- Rewarding to control

Strategy #3

EMPLOY THE 7 CONNECTING HABITS

Dr. William Glasser strongly suggests adults to eliminate the "Seven Deadly Habits" and start using the "Seven Connecting Habits" with teenagers. These positive habits will almost immediately strengthen relationships. Be patient. Your adolescent may be a bit suspicious at first but there will be positive changes if he or she sees that you are sincere.

THE SEVEN CONNECTING HABITS

- Caring
- Trusting
- Listening
- Supporting
- Negotiating
- Befriending
- Encouraging

Strategy #4

ATTACHED TO YOUR HIP

We often wonder why we see so many angry and unhappy adolescents. Could it be our fault? When they look at us, what do they see? Do they see happy adults who appear to enjoy their work or do they see moody, irritable, and miserable people who seem to be "just going through the motions" of everyday life?

In his book, *It's a Meaningful Life*, Bo Lozoff offers these thoughts. "If there was an invisible child or teenager attached to your hip, following you throughout the day, would he see somebody who is really enjoying the moments of who you are and what you're doing? Would he see somebody who would inspire him to say, 'I want what he's having,' or 'I can't wait to be a grown-up?' Would he see peace? Would he see a depth of joy and contentment, equanimity, a gracefulness about life?" (p. 138). If we don't smile or act like we enjoy our life and our job, what incentive is there for children to aspire to be successful academically? Some days it isn't easy to smile and appear content in our classrooms, but we must make a daily effort to let students know that, "Hey, being a teacher is an enjoyable profession and working with kids is neat!"

So, if there was an invisible child attached to your hip, what would he/she see? Students need to see us smile often. Thich Nhat Hanh, a world-renowned writer and poet reminds us, "Every time you smile away your irritation and anger, you achieve a victory for yourself and for humanity."

Strategy #5

DON'T FORGET TO WATER THE SEEDS

In his book, *Anger: Wisdom for Cooling the Flames*, Thich Nhat Hanh writes about watering seeds. We all know that flower seeds need watering in order to grow. Hanh believes that inside each individual are seeds of anger and seeds of love and compassion. If the seeds of anger are watered, the person will grow to be an unhappy, moody, angry adult. People, whose seeds of compassion are watered frequently, learn to be kind, loving, and caring. Every time we talk to a young person, we need to ask ourselves, "Am I watering his anger seeds or his compassion seeds?" I encourage teachers and parents to keep a small flower watering can (the kind with a long nozzle with holes in the end and a handle) on their desk, table, or shelf as a visual reminder to daily water the seeds of compassion in every young person.

Strategy #6

OBSERVING THE CEILING FAN

This may sound a bit silly or elementary, but I believe one of the best ways to understand and deal with anger is to observe a ceiling fan. First, as educators and parents, we need to do the following activity. Later we can teach it to young people.

- Find a comfortable chair and look up at the ceiling fan while it is off.

- Have someone turn it on.

- Notice how it starts off slowly and builds up to its top speed. This is like anger. It tends to build up inside people until it reaches top speed and they explode.

- When the fan is going full speed, you shouldn't try to touch it. When an angry person is going at full speed we probably shouldn't try to touch or deal him or her unless someone is getting hurt physically. When young people are very angry, they are seldom open to a discussion with an adult.

- After observing the fan at full speed, have someone turn it off.

- Notice when the fan switch is turned off, the fan doesn't stop immediately. Anger, also doesn't stop immediately.

- The fan may take a minute or two to finally stop. Even when the fan is slowing down, we shouldn't touch it. Just as a child is starting to calm down, we would best be advised to leave him/her alone.

- Once the ceiling fan has finally stopped, it can safely be touched. Once a child has finally calmed down, he or she will be more open to reason. Never try to open lines of communication with adolescents until they are under control of their emotions!

Strategy #7

SIGNING THE DECLARATION

Sometime during the first week or two of school, have a classroom discussion on the topic of tolerance. Encourage the class to sign the **Declaration of Tolerance** (Skill Sheet #2) and make two copies. Post one on the wall and send the other copy to the Southern Poverty Law Center, 400 Washington Avenue, Montgomery, Alabama 36104. The people at the Southern Poverty Law Center devised the declaration and encourage schools to send them signed copies as a promise to make a valid attempt to improve tolerance in our country. The more tolerant our students are, the less anger we'll see.

DECLARATION OF TOLERANCE

Tolerance is a personal decision that comes from a belief that every person is a treasure. I believe that America's diversity is its strength. I also recognize that ignorance, insensitivity and bigotry can turn that diversity into a source of prejudice and discrimination.

To help keep diversity a wellspring of strength and make America a better place for all, I pledge to have respect for people whose abilities, beliefs, culture, race, sexual identity, or other characteristics are different from my own.

To fulfill this pledge, I will.....

❑ Examine my own biases and work to overcome them,

❑ Set a positive example for my family and friends,

❑ Work for tolerance in my own community, and

❑ Speak out against hate and injustice.

SIGNATURES:

_____   _____   _____

_____   _____   _____

_____   _____   _____

_____   _____   _____

_____   _____   _____

_____   _____   _____

_____   _____   _____

This declaration was developed by the Southern Poverty Law Center in Montgomery, AL and used with permission.

Strategy #8

REMOVING THE BARRICADES

There are three types of barricades or "communication blockers" we must avoid using when talking with an angry student.

Judging:
By saying things like "You are wrong to feel that way" or "Calm down, it's nothing to get upset about," you can make the student feel defensive.

Trying to give suggestions too early:
Be quiet for a few minutes and listen. Angry people seldom want our advice; they just want to vent.

Avoiding:
If the angry person believes you aren't listening, he may get even more upset. Give eye contact and watch your body language.

Strategy #9

ANGRY MORNING MEETINGS

For over thirty years William Glasser has encouraged teachers to conduct morning Class Meetings as a way of improving classroom environments. If performed properly, these informal gatherings can prevent many discipline problems. It seems that numerous elementary teachers are utilizing Glasser's idea, but his suggested meetings are rarely found in middle and high schools. Upper grade level teachers will blame tight schedules and tough curriculums for not having enough time. Glasser will argue that Class Meetings will take up a little time in the mornings, but eventually they will help later on as there will be fewer discipline problems and disruptions because the teachers and students will have formed stronger/closer relationships.

Teachers of adolescents may benefit from finding a few minutes, daily or weekly, to have meetings. One topic to use often should be **anger**. Encourage students to share experiences in which they were victims of the anger of others. Besides talking about experiences and feelings, have students share strategies that helped them control their anger.

One of the best ways to start a Class Meeting on anger is to read a quote and then let the discussion begin. Here are a couple quotes to get you started.

> *"I will permit no man to narrow and degrade my soul by making me hate him."*
> — Booker T. Washington

> *"Anger cannot be overcome by anger. If a person shows anger to you, and you respond with anger, the result is disastrous. On contrast, if you control anger and show opposite attitudes—compassion, tolerance and patience—then not only do you yourself remain in peace, but the other's anger will gradually diminish."*
> — Dalai Lama

Strategy #10

GOT BOUNCE?

In 2004 the American Psychological Association developed a brochure especially for teens that provided tips to build resilience. Resilient teens are better prepared to handle stress and anger. The APA brochure goes by the title, "Got Bounce?" Provide all your students with an adapted version on Skill Sheet #3.

Strategy #11

THE PROFESSIONAL TOUCH

I remember the day very well: September 3, 2004. That was the day my son, who teaches in a middle school, brought me a note from his grade level principal that read, "Teachers are to refrain from touching any student for any reason as this action can be misinterpreted by the student." How sad! No longer would my son be allowed to greet his students in the morning with a firm handshake. No more "high fives" for a job well done. No more "pats" on the back. I wondered, was he allowed to hug a grieving child?

I've worked with hundreds of difficult adolescents. In order to make progress with them I had to build trust, truly listen, show compassion and eventually feel safe to shake their hands or pat them on the back. So many of our angry, hostile students are hurting emotionally. They are rarely "touched" in a positive way by their parents. I encourage teachers to proceed slowly and cautiously, but when the timing is right, give that needy adolescent a professional touch. If more and more parents and educators would show compassion and give an occasional touch to these hurting adolescents, then fewer of them would turn to drugs and gangs for attention.

GOT BOUNCE?*
TEN TIPS FOR TEENS TO BUILD RESILIENCE

Socialize.
Don't be a loner. Talk with friends, parents, teachers and others in your community.

Cut yourself some slack.
Accept the fact that bad things happen to everyone. Go easy on yourself and your friends.

Create a hassle-free zone.
Select a private setting to be alone when you begin to get stressed. Go to your room, climb a tree, or sit by the river.

Develop a plan.
What can you do when you get stressed? Develop a consistent plan or routine.

Take care of yourself.
Get enough sleep, exercise regularly, and watch what you eat. Are you fit physically, mentally, and spiritually?

Take control.
Even in the midst of tragedy, you can move toward goals one small step at a time. Bad times make us feel out of control. Grab some of that control back by taking decisive action.

Express yourself.
If talking doesn't work, do something else to capture your emotions—start a journal or create art.

Help others.
One of the best ways to forget about your problems is to help others.

Put things in perspective.
Learn some relaxation techniques. Try meditation, yoga, or deep breathing. Don't let the little things get you down. Think of the real important things in life like friends, family, your religion, and community.

Turn it off.
Stay informed—you may even have homework that requires you to watch the news, but try to limit the amount of news you take in, whether from newspapers, television, magazines, or the Internet.

This list is adapted from the American Psychological Association's brochure, "Got Bounce?" and the April, 2004 issue of Spirituality & Health.

Strategy #12

STOP TALKING TO THE WALL

It's no secret to middle school teachers that students spend a great deal of time gossiping, complaining, and talking about their peers. Many of these negative habits can lead to teasing, shoving, and fights. I've spent much time trying to tell these students that it is a waste of time. You can't change others; you can only change yourself. Complaining about others is like talking to the wall. I read an article one time that said twelve-year-old girls spend an average of eight hours a week talking/gossiping about their peers (telephone calls, emails, lunch, bus rides, traveling in the halls, etc). If this is true, multiply 8 hours a week times 52 weeks and you'll discover they spend over 400 hours a year talking about others!

Following is a quote I often use with students who tend to spend too much time talking, gossiping, and complaining about others. Consider posting it in our room.

You can't change others.
You can only change yourself.
But, when you change,
They change.

Strategy #13

CLASSY CLASSICAL CLASSROOM MUSIC

More and more middle and high school teachers tell me they play soft, classical music in the background during study time. At first, students laugh at the music and call it "stupid." But after a while they get use to it and actually admit they like its calming affect. Many of these teachers truly feel that the music helps prevent behavior problems such as talking, and arguing. It also lowers stress and helps with concentration.

Strategy #14

24 DESKS & 3 STATIONARY BIKES

I believe that one of the best investments a teacher could make would be to purchase two or three used stationary bikes to put in the back of the classroom. Let me tell you why.

- So many children today are ADHD, fidgety, hyper, and full of excess energy. Let these kids pedal for five or ten minutes and watch the improvement in behavior and attention.

- When a student begins to get angry, let him hop on the bike and pedal hard for a few minutes. He can pedal the anger away.

- Because of testing requirements, students are getting less playtime and exercise. Let the students take turns pedaling. They can still read a book while biking!

- Biking and other forms of exercise pumps oxygen to the brain. The more oxygen, the better the brain works.

- Students can set goals such as trying to bike 100 miles for the semester.

Strategy #15

THE ELEVEN MOST IMPORTANT WORDS

In his book, *The Four Things That Matter Most*, Dr. Ira Byock tells of the many experiences he's had with dying patients. He writes that many people, on the verge of death, often have regrets about things they wished they had said to significant others in their lives. Byock refers to this as unfinished business. Parents and teachers are encouraged to use the following words often with those they truly care about. Byock labels them as "the eleven most important words." Use these words often. Avoid having unfinished business.

Please forgive me.
> **I forgive you.**
>> **Thank you.**
>>> **I love you.**

Strategy #16

THE POWER OF PICKLES

Parents and teachers often reward good behavior with sweet tasting goodies like chocolate bars, gum, hard candy, or cookies. Have you ever heard of anyone using pickles as a reward? I have, **and** it works with middle schoolers!

After presenting a workshop on anger I had a participant come up front to share his successful pickle program. The gentleman had taught seventh grade for over twenty years. He noted that his students seemed to enjoy sour tasting items rather than sweet. He also observed their eating habits in the cafeteria and was amazed at how many enjoyed feasting on large dill pickles. He decided to experiment with a new incentive program.

One Monday he brought a large jar of dill pickles to class. Throughout the week he would pass out pickle coupons to students who achieved various behavioral or academic goals. The students could redeem the coupons and use the tongs to pull a pickle out of the jar. The teacher was extremely surprised at the popularity of his new program. The students **loved** sour pickles! This creative teacher discovered that the students who were helped the most were those with anger problems and attention problems. There was something about the sour flavor hitting/awakening the taste buds that helped these special students stay calm and focused.

The teacher told me how much the students liked his class and how behavior problems decreased. He remembered a time one of his students said to him, "Other teachers give out candy, pencils, stickers, or homework passes, but you are the only one who gives us pickles!" One year his class members chipped in and bought him a pickle necktie.

I was fascinated by his program so I decided to do an experiment. When fourth and fifth graders visited my office I offered them the choice of a sweet snack or pickle. Nearly 75% wanted the pickle! Can pickles help with behavior problems? I think so. Also, it is good to know that pickles are good for you and they have almost no calories.

Strategy #17

FOUR FACTS THAT ALL PARENTS MUST KNOW

Recently I've completed much research on the topic of Conduct Disorder. Over and over my findings all come back to the four following preventive measures that help to greatly reduce the possibilities of a child displaying the characteristics of this devastating disorder.

- Firm boundaries and leadership by the father
- Warmth, involvement, and consistency from the mother
- Parents that display affection toward each other
- Families that do activities together

I believe that these four facts will not only help with Conduct Disorder, they will help parents prevent many anger problems. Counselors, therapists, school psychologists, and social workers may wish to write articles in the school newsletter or conduct parenting workshops that stress the above four facts.

Strategy #18

YOU KNOW WHERE THE TRASH GOES

Middle school students often bring "outside" problems into the classroom. When they get upset they occasionally start talking "trash" to classmates. What to do? Place a large trash barrel near the door. Remind students that you have a "no trash allowed" rule. Students are encouraged to visually put their trash in the barrel. Some teachers may ask the vocal students to write their trash words on a piece of paper and place it in the barrel. Hopefully when students see the trash barrel, they'll settle down. One other suggestion is to have students paint the trash barrel or write some clever, positive graffiti on the exterior.

Strategy #19

READ THEM THEIR RIGHTS

Many of our adolescents get in to trouble because they end up "in the wrong place at the wrong time." We need to coach them on how to monitor their environments. Adolescents must constantly be aware of who they are with and where they are. By self-monitoring, they can prevent many problems. See Skill Sheet #4. Make copies and place them in locations where young people tend to gather. Maybe these postings will help remind young people to make the right choices.

ASK YOURSELF
AM I ...

*IN THE
RIGHT PLACE?*

*AT THE
RIGHT TIME?*

*WITH THE
RIGHT PEOPLE?*

*DOING THE
RIGHT THING?*

Strategy #20

IN PURSUIT OF HAPPINESS

So many of our angry and depressed adolescents have a tendency to always blame others for their problems. They seldom take action to improve their situation. A few years ago, Jeff Bezos, Amazon.com CEO and founder, wrote an eye-opening article that we should all think about. His article which appeared in the book, *250 Ways to Make America Better*, urged adults to encourage young people to be more responsible for their own well being and happiness. He wrote:

Read the Declaration of Independence to your children. Do it as a tradition every Fourth of July, maybe just after they've had their fill of hot dogs and hamburgers. Discuss it with them; ask questions. Make sure they understand why the word "pursuit" precedes the word "happiness." (p. 94).

Ask yourself the following questions. Do I tolerate adolescents always blaming others? Do I encourage them to be more responsible for their feelings? Do I acknowledge their progress? Do I keep them updated about clubs, sports, and other programs that they can participate in at school? Do I go to watch and support them at their games and other performances? The more we can get young people to pursue happiness, the less anger we should see.

Strategy #21

THE DANGERS OF SMOKING, DRINKING, DRUGS, AND ANGER

Schools do a decent job of teaching students about the dangers of tobacco, drinking too much alcohol, and taking illegal drugs. Most students know how these habits can affect their health, but very few know how anger affects health. Find time to make "Anger and Health Related Issues" part of the middle and high school curriculum. In the book, *The Anger Management Sourcebook*, authors Schiraldi and Kerr mention the long-term health problems of not controlling one's anger.

Those prone to anger, hostility, and/or aggression are at a higher risk for high blood pressure, coronary heart disease, stroke, death from all causes, and job injuries. They might be at a greater risk for headaches, backaches, cancer, ulcers, and gastrointestinal disturbance. They are more likely to smoke and relapse from psychological illness. In post-traumatic stress disorder, anger hinders the processing of trauma and is associated with symptom severity following exposure to traumatic events. People who are prone to anger tend to oversecrete stress hormones (cortisol and catecholamines), which damage heart muscles and the cells lining blood vessels, make blood platelets stickier, weaken the immune system, and raise cholesterol. Disrupted relationships and loneliness are also associated with greater risk of heart disease.

(p. 20-21)

Strategies #22-24

THE CALMING PATHS OF LABYRINTHS

Up until recently, the only place you would find a labyrinth was at a church. Nowadays they are being found on school playgrounds, college campuses, hospitals, and prisons. Doctors, teachers, counselors, and other professionals are discovering the calming affects of walking the labyrinth. What is a labyrinth? An excellent description comes from Melissa Gayle West's book, *Exploring the Labyrinth*:

> *A labyrinth is different from a maze, though the two are often confused. The labyrinth is one of the oldest contemplative and transformational tools known to humankind, used for centuries for prayer, ritual, initiation, and spiritual growth. This ancient and powerful tool is unicursal, offering only one route to the center and back out again: no blinds alleys, dead ends, or tricks, as in a maze. No matter where you are in the labyrinth's coherent circuits you can always see the center. Once you set your foot upon its path, the labyrinth gently and faultlessly leads you to the center of both the labyrinth and yourself, no matter how many twists and turns you negotiate in the process. Since the destination is assured, there are no obstacles to overcome, no muddles to figure out, no dead ends to retrace.* (p. 4-5).

I strongly believe that the labyrinth can be a very powerful tool for helping people with anger problems. Study the next three strategies and consider how you might implement the use of a labyrinth in your school or classroom.

Strategy #22

THE WALKING LABYRINTH

If your school yard is big enough, consider constructing a walking labyrinth. There are several books available on how to build one and they are not expensive. Students will enjoy building one out of rocks, sand, sticks, and lumber. Parents may help in the construction and donate material. I suggest you place a bench at the center of the labyrinth where students can sit and think before retracing their paths. Students should slowly walk the path alone, but I have seen situations where two students who had a conflict, walked together in an attempt to resolve their issues.

If you don't have the outdoor space, you might want to purchase a cloth or plastic labyrinth that you can fold and unfold and place on a large floor space such as the gym. Walking a labyrinth does wonders to help calm an angry student.

Strategy #23

THE LABYRINTH TABLE

Purchase a quality wooden labyrinth that can be placed on small table in the corner of your classroom. Instruct all the students on how to use it. Students should be allowed to use it when they feel a need to clam down and relax. Students with anger problems can be directed to utilize the board as a preventive measure.

Here are some basic instructions for using the labyrinth.

- Sit comfortably at the table.

- Sit quietly. No talking, humming, etc.

- Place your index finger in the groove at the start of the labyrinth.

- Close your eyes.

- Slowly move your finger along the path.

- Concentrate of the smooth, soft feel of the board.

- When you reach the center, pause to think about your concerns, problems, frustrations.

- Slowly retrace your path back to the start/finish point.

Strategy #24

INDIVIDUAL DESKTOP FINGER LABYRINTHS

Give students a copy of Skill Sheet #5 and let them design their own desk top labyrinth. Play sand may also be used as a media.

DESK TOP FINGER LABYRINTH

Directions: Lightly color the path of your personal labyrinth. Use soft colors such as yellow, light blue or light green. Do not color over the black lines; you need to see the path. Next, cut out your labyrinth and paste it on a thick piece of cardboard or a thin piece of wood. Store it under your desk. Bring it out, with a teacher's permission, and use it to help you unwind and think about your behavior or personal problems. Remember, travel the path slowly with your index finger. Pause at the center and then retrace your path.

Strategies #25-34

ANGRY ADOLESCENT EYES

Whenever you see angry adolescents, study their eyes. Their eyes can tell us many things. The following ten "eye" strategies can help you to better understand and deal with an angry and defiant adolescent.

Strategy #25

CRYING EYES

Inside many angry adolescents is a lot of hurt. When some of these teens get upset, they may not express their emotions with anger, but they may express it with tears instead. Let these teens know that it is alright to cry. Crying can be a very healthy release. I tell students that when they cry, it washes their eyes so they can see better. Crying can be a wonderful release and afterward there can be a sense of peace and relaxation that travels throughout the whole body. In his book, *Thank You for Being Such a Pain*, Mark Rosen writes, "Scientists have found that when tears are shed for emotional reasons, they have a different chemical make-up than they do when the eyes are simply irritated. Crying is a natural mechanism for the release of emotion. People who can't or won't cry are not taking advantage of an important emotional outlet." (p. 156).

Give your students a safe environment to release their emotions. Listen to their hurt and always keep a box of tissues close by.

Strategy #26

"OH THOSE ROLLING EYES"

It usually doesn't take a young person very long to discover certain behaviors that really irritate us. Too many of us adults, the "rolling of the eyes" when we are talking to an angry or defiant child ranks near the top of our list of what we may consider disrespectful behavior. Some teachers and parents can ignore this behavior and go on with the reprimand while others become extremely agitated. When an adolescent rolls his eyes, it doesn't necessarily mean that he doesn't respect you. He may just be trying to "be cool" around his peers. I recommend that you stay calm and continue your conversation. The worse thing you can do is to let the child know that you are getting angry. If this happens, he gains power and senses that he can control your emotions.

Strategy #27

EYES LOOK UP TO CALM DOWN

I had the privilege to attend one of Ruby Payne's fascinating workshops called, "A Framework for Understanding Poverty." During the question and answer period a teacher asked Ruby if she had any tricks for calming an angry student. Ruby replied, "Tell the angry student to look up at the ceiling or sky for a few seconds." Ruby noted that when a student does this, his/her anger lessens. It is hard to explain why it works, but it does! Give it a try.

Strategy #28

LOOK ME IN THE EYES WHEN I'M TALKING TO YOU!

Probably one of the worse things we can do when talking with an angry adolescent is to say, "Look me in the eyes when I'm speaking to you!" Yes, looking at each other during a conversation is important and it should be discussed occasionally during Character Education, but it is not wise to bring it up during heat of battle. You can't force a student to look you in the eye and I strongly advise that you don't grab their chin and try to turn the student's face towards yours. Even if the student does not give you eye contact, continue your talk and keep your message short.

One other note here about eye contact. Every year our country is becoming more culturally diverse. We need to do our homework and become aware of the various customs of the countries from which our students come. In many cultures around the world, it is not considered disrespectful to look away when an adult speaks.

Strategy #29

FIGHTING EYES

If you ever witness two students getting ready to fight, if possible, study their eyes. I believe that most of the time one of the students doesn't really want to fight. Once you make your presence known, see which of the students looks at you. If neither one looks at you then there could be a big battle brewing. If one of the students looks at you, then that is usually the one who wishes not to fight and may welcome a rescue. So if you do intervene, go for the one who gives you eye contact.

Many years ago there was a well-known European psychologist named Kenneth Strongman who had a similar philosophy as mine when it comes to witnessing two potential combatants. He said that when two people stare at each other, the one who looks away first is the dominator. Strongman believes this may be true because the stronger person is afraid of causing harm by staring too long, obscurely aware of the force and the powers of the eye and of the weak defenses of the person sitting or standing opposite. He stated, "Only people with a superior moral sense look away (which is partly what makes them dominators) while the wicked, feeling strong, will never look away."

Strategy #30
LINEBACKER EYES

In football, probably the most difficult position to play is linebacker. Unlike other positions on defense, the linebacker has to study the whole field at all times. If he thinks the offence is going to pass, he must drop back and hope for an interception. If it looks like a running play he must fill the hole and hope for a tackle. Years ago there was a famous linebacker named Michael Singletary who played for the Chicago Bears. There are many pictures of him staring at the offence. He has become famous for his "linebacker eyes."

Angry adolescents seldom have linebacker eyes. When they get upset they tend to focus on one person or thing; they don't search around (like a linebacker does) to study the situation or to hear the whole story. We need to encourage our adolescents to be patient, gather the facts, look around, and not react hastily.

Also, I need to remind teachers and parents to acquire linebacker eyes. Adults must do their best to not over react and to gather all the facts before confronting an adolescent.

Strategy #31
DECEPTIVE EYES

Although this book focuses on adolescents with anger problems, let's not forget those quiet, shy, withdrawn students. On the outside they appear unlikely to be candidates for having anger outbursts but, on the inside, many of them are dealing with some heavy-duty issues. Some may be victims of bullying, neglect, and/or abuse. Often these students attempt to be strong and suppress their emotions, but eventually, some may suddenly explode. News reports from recent years have reported that many of the most violent acts in schools (i.e., shootings) have been committed by the less obvious students. Be sure to carefully monitor the behaviors and actions of all your students. Don't assume the quiet child is always doing fine.

Strategy #32
DON'T LET THEM PULL THE WOOL OVER YOUR EYES

Adolescents are pretty crafty at times. They may appear to be angry when they really aren't. Many have learned that they receive a lot of attention from others when they are angry. Friends and adults gather around. The next time you encounter an angry student, be sure he/she isn't pulling the wool over your eyes and his friends' eyes.

The origin of this cliché is interesting. It involves deception, and "pulling" is *pull the wool over (someone's) eyes*. Many years ago in England people wore massive wigs on their heads. Purse snatchers would literally pull the wool wigs over the eyes of their victims and take their money.

Strategy #33

COMPUTER EYES

Many adolescents today have what I call, "computer eyes." They have a blank stare and show little, if any, empathy. I believe they get that way from hundreds of hours of looking at video games, computer screens, and television. So much of what they watch is violent and can negatively affect their behaviors. The September 16, 2003 issue of the *Washington Post* reported, "More than 70 percent of American teenage boys have played the violent but popular "Grand Theft Auto" video games, and they are more likely to have been in a fight than those who have not played, according to a new Gallup Poll released on Tuesday. The poll also found that 62 percent of teenagers play games at least one hour a week, while 25 percent play six or more hours per week." The American Academy of Pediatrics reported on a study done at Wake Forest University in 2001. They noted that frequency of watching wrestling on television positively correlated with increased date fighting and health risk behaviors. The study also correlated increased fighting, weapon and gun carrying, non-prescription Ritalin use, and driving after drinking.

Parents must monitor what their children are watching. Sometimes children see so much violence on the screen that they have trouble figuring out what is real and what is fiction. Teachers must limit computer time at school and closely monitor the websites students are viewing.

Strategy #34

TRUTHFUL EYES

After Jenny finally settles down, invite her to talk. Remind her that anger is a normal feeling that needs to be vented in acceptable ways. But she also must know that the angry feelings need to be addressed with honesty. Encourage her to look you in the eyes and to speak truthfully about the issues that are causing her to get upset. I usually tell a student to be honest because, "Your eyes don't lie."

Here is a neat quote I've seen posted in classrooms. Read it. Think about it. Does it make sense to you? Ask your students to share their thoughts about it.

REAL EYES
REALIZE
REAL LIES

CATEGORY 2:
MODERATE ANGER

Strategy #35

HEAVY STONES IN THEIR BACKPACKS

In his book, *Thank You for the Pain*, Mark I. Rosen notes, "Almost all difficult behaviors result from suffering, deprivation, or ignorance. People do the things they do to other people because they hurt, they want, and they don't know." Many of our angry, difficult adolescents are hurting; they are carrying a lot of pain. Many have no father in the house while others have dealt with abuse, neglect, teasing and bullying. Often these hurting children deal with their emotions by striking out at others.

Let us consider the "backpack analogy." Every student has a backpack on his/her back. Inside each one are heavy stones. Each stone represents one hurt or pain in their lives. Some lucky students have very few, if any, stones. Others, like Alex, have several heavy stones weighing them down. Alex's mother died when he was two. His father is an alcoholic and because he is rather small, he has been a frequent target of bullies. Alex also struggles with a learning disability. Alex's backpack is very heavy. Will he get depressed and give up on life or will he resort to using anger as a coping skill?

One of our roles as educators is to help students remove some of the heavy stones. The lighter their backpack, the more likely they'll be successful. How do we do it? Most of the time it can be done with words. Here are a few examples.

- "John, how is your grandmother doing in the hospital?"

- "Shaneeka, you showed a lot of patience working with that kindergartener."

- "Cynthia, your presentation was great!"

- "Bo, I'm sorry about your mother. Do you need a few extra days to complete your project?"

- "LuAnn, you are fast! Have you ever thought about trying out for track?"

- "Tim, I enjoy having you in class."

- "Otis, which CD's are you listening to these days?"

Remember, each kind word and act of compassion removes a stone.

Strategy #36

THOUGHT STOPPING

Many of the anger management strategies we teach young people are often lengthy procedures. For instance, we may suggest counting colors, taking deep breaths, walking a labyrinth, or chanting mantras. These strategies are effective, but there will be times when adolescents need to use a quicker, more direct tool. One such tool is known as "thought stopping." When anger producing thoughts enter the mind, some people may have to use the direct approach of saying to themselves, "Stop!" They can say it quietly or in some instances they can shout it out loud. This strategy has one meeting the negative feeling head-on. Quite often this will make the negative thoughts disappear. Encourage adolescents to use thought stopping when time is an issue.

Strategy #37

THE "MUST AVOID" WORD

Try your best to avoid using the word "why" when confronting an angry student. When a student has misbehaved, and you ask why, you are giving the student an opportunity to come up with a valid reason (in his eyes) why he did what he did. For example, if you ask Alphonzo **why** he hit Bruce, I can almost guarantee that he'll respond by saying something like, "He hit me first!" If you ask Shirley **why** she doesn't have her homework, she'll say, "Oh, I left it at home. I'll bring it tomorrow." Adolescents always seem to have a good reason why they do what they do. Let's not give them a chance to create clever excuses. There's an old Sufi saying that goes, "Self-justification is worse than the original offence."

Also, if you encounter an extremely angry adolescent and ask, "Why are you angry?" he or she will probably blame others for his/her anger. The student will say something like, "Adam made me mad when he made fun of my new shirt."

Instead of using the word **why**, use **what**. Here are some examples.

- "What happened?"

- "What did you do?"

- "What is the class rule about turning in homework assignments?"

- "What are you supposed to do when someone pushes you?"

- "What else could you have done?"

By encouraging the use of the word **what**, it becomes a strategy to help students become more responsible for their actions. Remember, no excuses!

Strategy #38

SKIP, SKIP, SKIP TO MY LOO...

Several years ago I visited a middle school near Chicago. I arrived early and was given permission to tour the building on my own. When the bell rang, signifying the end of fifth period, hundreds of students rushed into the hall, almost knocking me over. As typical of most middle schoolers there was a lot of "trash" talk, gossiping, teasing, pushing and shoving. I saw very few smiles. At the start of the sixth period I stopped by the gym to observe a physical education class. The teacher had her class of thirty-three sixth graders line up in a circle. When the whistle blew, the students started skipping around the gym. Almost immediately, all the students, even the big tough boys, were laughing and giggling. After two or three minutes of skipping the teacher had them stop and then gave them instructions for the rest of the period. I saw almost no discipline problems.

At the end of the day I asked the physical education teacher if I could ask her a few questions about her skipping routine. She was more than happy to share information. As best as my memory allows, here is a brief synopsis of her comments.

> *Early in my career I realized how difficult middle schoolers could be. Many of them were full of anger and defiant. I had a hard time keeping my classes under control. Then one day I saw a group of older adults at a nursing home skipping; they were all smiling and having a good time. Soon I observed people of all ages, from kindergarten to those at the nursing home, and realized that when they were skipping, they were happy. Have you ever seen anyone frown or act grumpy while skipping? I soon started my skipping program with all the students in grades 6-8. They love it. There are very few "bad" attitudes in gym. Fighting, teasing, and bullying just don't happen. There are three or four other teachers here that have their students skipping.*

Consider a skipping program with your students. It might not be a bad idea to get teachers skipping before faculty meetings!

Strategy #39

EXPLORING THE 10 S'S

Many adolescents have so much stress in their lives that it can lead them towards anger problems. They need to self-monitor their stress levels. I recommend that middle and high school students do a stress self audit three or four times a year. Give all of your students a copy of Skill Sheet #6: "The Student Stress Self-Audit: Exploring the 10 S's."

Note: The ten items on this stress scale include factors that, for the most part, adolescents have some ability to control. We must understand that many adolescents live in very stressful homes in which they have little or no control (i.e. too strict parents, drug abuse by parents, poverty, illness, divorce, etc.).

STUDENT STRESS SELF AUDIT
Exploring the 10 S's

Directions: Rate yourself on each of the ten areas of stress.　　Today's date _____

5- **I'm doing great in this area**　　　2- **I could do much better in this area**
4- **Overall, I'm doing ok**　　　　　　1- **I'm really hurting in this area, much**
3- **Not too bad. I could do a better job**　　　**room for improvement**
　　　　　　　　　　　　　　　　　　　0- **I've hit bottom here, doing poorly**

AREAS	DESCRIPTIONS	RATING
SLEEP	I am getting enough sleep. I feel fresh and rested and energized. On most school nights I get at least eight hours of sleep.	_____
STUDIES	I can honestly say I'm doing the best I can. I'm doing quality work. I complete assignments and study for exams.	_____
SUSTENANCE	I watch what I eat, not too much junk food. I eat a good breakfast every morning. I eat enough fruit and vegetables.	_____
SOLITUDE	Almost every day I try to find quiet time for myself. I sit quietly in my room or go outdoors.	_____
SPORTS	I get plenty of exercise. I play a team sport or I exercise alone by running, walking, swimming, or biking.	_____
SERVICE	Every week I find time to help others. I volunteer through my school or church. I do things to improve my community.	_____
SPIRITUALITY	I find time to attend the religious institution of my choice. I take time to appreciate nature, the earth, and sun. I feel blessed.	_____
SOCIAL LIFE	I have several friends and at least one "real close" friend who is always there for me. I attend social events on a regular basis.	_____
SUN	I get outdoors often to soak up the valuable rays of the sun. I like going outside to read, play, relax, or exercise.	_____
SUBSTANCES	I limit my intake of caffeine. I avoid smoking, alcohol, and illegal drugs. I do not abuse prescription drugs.	_____

TOTAL POINTS: [　　]

Scoring

40-50 points: Stress level low.　20-29 points: A little bit high, 　10-19 points: Stress level high.　Less than 10 points: Extremely
30-39 points: Stress level average.　　　monitor closely.　　　　　　　　　　　　　　　　　high, seek assistance.

Strategy #40

THE MOOD TREE

One of our goals is to help adolescents monitor their own feelings. They need tools to help them keep an eye on changes in their emotions in order to prevent anger episodes. The Mood Tree is one of the tools that children and young adolescents seem to enjoy using. According to the book, *The Bipolar Child*, "The Mood Tree is a personal and customized graphic representation of a child's moods, feelings, and actions at a particular point in time. This tangible communication tool is rather like a board game with Colorform-like apples. These apples can be chosen by the child and placed on the tree to illustrate what he or she is feeling." (p. 158).

The Mood Tree has proven to be very useful for both parents and therapists who work with young people. The Mood Tree is available in both child and adolescent versions.

Strategy #41

STRESS DOTS

Another emotion monitoring tool that older adolescents have told me is "cool" goes by the name Biodots. Biodots, created by Bob Grabhorn, are self-adhesive dots (about the size of a hole punch) that adhere to the back of your hand. They are heat sensitive and change color in response to stress. This makes a rudimentary biofeedback device. People are encouraged to wear one for a day to find out who, or what, causes them stress. Black means stressed while blue means you are relaxed.

For more information about Biodots, write to:
Stresstop, 3 Morning Side Pl., Norwalk, CT 06854

Strategy #42

NEVERTHELESS

Many adolescents reach a point in their lives in which they truly believe their behaviors and misbehaviors are justified. They always seem to come up with valid reasons (in their eyes) why they don't have their homework completed or why it was only fair to "hit him back." Research and personal experience find that we should avoid arguing with an angry adolescent. We will not win the argument, but we **can** stick to the rules, be consistent, listen, express empathy, and avoid power struggles.

When confronting an argumentative student, try the "nevertheless" strategy. After he or she comes up with a weak reason or excuse for his or her actions, begin your response with "nevertheless." You will not be disagreeing with the student and you will not be giving in. This is a lot like the "broken record" approach. Following is an example.

Mrs. T:	Larry, you pushed Cindy!
Larry:	Ya, but she crowded ahead of me!
Mrs. T:	Nevertheless, pushing is against our rules.
Larry:	You're not fair! You always take her side.
Mrs. T:	Nevertheless, you owe her an apology.
Larry:	My dad said that I have a right to push her. She's always bugging me.
Mrs. T:	Nevertheless, you need to apologize.
Larry:	Why should I apologize, she started it!
Mrs. T:	Nevertheless, apologize or else you'll miss ten minutes free time.

Strategy #43

HANDY FRAGRANCES

Schools today are doing a better job of stressing the importance of washing hands several times daily. We all know that dirty hands spread germs and cause illness. It is not uncommon to see "Wash hands!" signs in the bathrooms and bottles of liquid soaps on teachers' desks. Here is a strategy that can assist teachers in two ways. One, it will help keep many students from acquiring germs that will make them ill. Secondly, this strategy reduces stress and anger in the classroom.

Keep several bottles of pleasant smelling antibacterial liquid soaps in your room. Some fragrances to consider are lavender, peach, strawberry, and wintergreen. A couple times a day, pick up a bottle and travel up and down the aisles. Students wishing to have soap will hold out their hands. I believe that most students will accept a squeeze from the bottle. They seem to enjoy breathing in the calming aromas and they get excited by experiencing different fragrances. Also, the rubbing of the hands together as they "wash," burns off nervous energy. Try this strategy. I think you'll be amazed by how much the students enjoy it, and you'll have fewer anger episodes. Your students should also experience less stress.

Strategy #44

ANGER IS LIKE A BOOMERANG

Here's a quick activity to help young people realize the negative consequences of not keeping their anger under control. Have your students answer the following questions:

- **What is "The Golden Rule?"**

- **What is a boomerang?**

- **How is anger like a boomerang?**

    Notes: It amazes me how many young people do not know what "The Golden Rule" is. There are many variations of this rule. Here's the one I use.
    Treat other people the way you would like them to treat you.

    Here is the description of the word "boomerang" Webster's Dictionary:
    "a curved hardwood missile used by the natives of Australia, so balanced that, when thrown to a distance, it returns towards the thrower; an act that recoils on the agent"

Strategy #45

LOOK OUT FOR MISMATCHES

Adolescents are good at interpreting our body language and studying the tone of our voice. If our tone of voice and body language do not match, it can send a confusing message to the adolescent. For instance, if you talk politely to Joe but you are clenching your fist, what mixed message are you sending? If you are laughing and joking with a co-worker at the same time you say to Shawn, "You need to sit down or else I'll send you to the office." Does Shawn take you seriously? Avoid mismatches!

Strategy #46

IN SEARCH OF SLEEP

Americans are not getting enough sleep today. Studies show that most people are sleeping an hour less per night than a generation ago, two or three hours less per night than was standard in previous centuries, according to author and researcher, Gregg Easterbrook. The sleep researcher William Dement maintains that "If Americans and Europeans would simply go to bed an hour earlier each night, and turn off the television no later than an hour before that, Western society would be happier and healthier." (p. 197).

Adolescents are not getting enough sleep and it affects them behaviorally and academically. Lack of sleep makes them more irritable, moody, and prone to bouts of anger. Teachers have very little control over sleep issues. It is the parents' job to make sure their children are getting enough sleep. Please share a copy of Skill Sheet #7 with your parents.

HELPING YOUR CHILDREN IN THEIR "SEARCH FOR SLEEP"

- Adolescents need a minimum of eight or nine hours of sleep on school nights.

- Don't assume that when your child goes to bed at nine o'clock that he is sleeping. Some children are so "wound-up" from viewing television or playing video games that it may take two or three hours to fall asleep. Those who watch television right up to bedtime tend to have less deep sleep.

- Reading is the ideal before bedtime activity. Let your adolescent go to his room at nine o'clock, but allow him to read 30-60 minutes before lights out.

- Do not allow children to drink beverages with caffeine during and after dinner.

- Make sure adults turn down the television and use quiet voices after children are sent off to bed.

- Consider removing the television from their bedrooms.

- Try these suggestions for those children with severe sleep disorders.
  - ❑ Place an air or sound machine in their room. The sounds of a brook or stream can be very calming.

  - ❑ Check with your doctor about using magnesium for muscle relaxation.

  - ❑ Have them drink a cup of chamomile tea before going to bed. Chamomile is one of the safest medicinal herbs. It is a soothing, gentle relaxant and it has a satisfying, apple-like aroma and flavor. The name comes from the Greek kamai melon, meaning, ground apple.

  - ❑ Place a drop of lavender oil on his/her pillow.

  - ❑ Talk with your doctor about the possible use of melatonin.

- Set up an incentive program with your adolescent. If they maintain a regular bedtime routine they can earn special weekend privileges.

- Don't let your adolescents sleep "too" late on Saturday and Sunday.

- Allow your children to stay up late on weekdays two or three times a year for special events such as New Year's Eve, the World Series, presidential election, or music award shows.

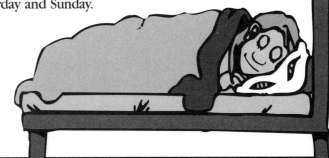

Strategy #47

THE TWO-MINUTE WARNING WHISTLE

Many easily angered students have trouble with transitions. I've witnessed students, as the bell rings, get all upset as they gather their material together. They are thinking, "Oh, no, I'm going to miss the bus," or "I'm going to get locked out of fifth period!" I've seen others, so engrossed in their work, that they were totally unaware the period was coming to an end. When the period came to the end, they were determined not to leave until their work was finished. They directed angry comments at the teachers for not letting them know time was almost up.

Now, I'm not suggesting you blow the two-minute warning whistle like the officials do in a football game, but you might want to consider some sound (i.e. buzzer, bell, verbal reminder) as the end of the period nears. It may prevent some anger outbursts.

Strategy #48

STOP PASSING ON THE PAIN

"If we could read the secret history of those we would like to punish, we would find in each life enough grief and suffering to make us stop wishing anything more on them."

— anonymous

"Be kind, for everyone you meet is fighting a hard battle."

— Philo

It is true. Many of our angry adolescents are trying their best to hide their emotional pain. Many have been abused, neglected, or have experienced violence, drugs, and poverty in their homes. Others don't have a father in the house and unfortunately a small number have never been told by a parent, "I love you." Some students have learning problems or are teased for being overweight. Often their pain begins to build like a volcano and eventually they explode. I believe that some of the "hurt" students experience is from jealousy when they see happy peers. They think to themselves, "It's not fair that their lives are great. I'm going to tease, bully, or spread rumors about them so they can feel pain in their lives just like I do." These angry students attempt to pass on their pain to others.

When I discuss this concept with students I use a football analogy. When someone throws the football to us, we are supposed to catch it. This is called a complete pass. When people try to pass on their pain to us, we do not want to catch it. We strive for an incomplete pass. We must stop the cycle of passing on pain to others. Just because someone is rude to us, we shouldn't be rude to others.

One final note here for parents and teachers who become targets of adolescent anger; don't take it personally. Think about the words of Tich Nhat Hanh, "When someone insults you or behaves violently towards you, you have to be intelligent enough to see that the person suffers from his own violence, anger, and pain."

Strategy #49

STOP TRYING TO MAKE EVERY CHILD A TEAM PLAYER

Have you ever seen a help wanted ad that stated, "Must be a team player?" I have, and I would never want to work in a place where I am coerced to be a team player. Team players tend not to be very creative, seldom question authority, and do not want to "rock the boat." Some of the most notable people in history were not team players. Rosa Parks, Martin Luther King, Jr., and Gandhi were not team players. They were not afraid to take a stand for what they believed in. They faced criticism and in some cases, they were actually jailed, but continued to persevere. Aren't you glad they were not team players?

Have you ever encountered a student who always wanted to do things "his way?" Did he ask questions like, "Why do we have to do it like that?" or "Hey, I've got a great suggestion. Do you want to hear it?" How do you react to students like this? Do you get defensive and annoyed or do you enjoy the challenge? If you constantly try to quiet this type of student or if you tell him, "No, I'm the teacher and I'm telling you that this is the only way we will do it," he may get angry and become a discipline problem. Instead of getting more authoritarian you may want to respond differently. Try, "Jake, do you have a better suggestion?" or "Benny, now that's a unique way of looking at that problem. Let me think about it for a while."

I had an eighth grader named Alex. I loved having him in my class. He made each day quite interesting as he asked tough questions and attempted to do things his way. The teacher across the hall truly disliked Alex and told me how much of a behavior problem he was most days. Alex became a very successful lawyer. Draw out each student's unique personality and do your best not to get too defensive when they ask, "Why do we always have to do it this way?"

Strategy #50

THE 24 HOUR RULE

As we all know, adolescents can be very moody and temperamental. In class on Monday Connie is quiet and well-behaved. On Tuesday she is very talkative and silly. On Wednesday she wears an angry face. Almost every adolescent has episodes of anger. I suggest that teachers use the "24 Hour Rule" when it comes to anger. If Matt is angry in class on Thursday and remains that way on Friday, you might consider some type of intervention. Even a simple, "Hey, Matt, how are doing today?" can open the door to some productive interaction.

Strategy #51

THE MORE YOU DO, THE MORE YOU'LL BE CRITICIZED

Ask your students this question: "What person in our country usually receives the most criticizing, ridicule, complaints, and is the target of jokes?" The answer: our president. Here's the point of this question. Usually the more things a person does, the more he or she is open to criticism. Adolescents must realize that when they run for Student Council President, play two sports, join 4-H, work hard to make the Honor Roll, or become a conflict manager, they open themselves to possible criticism from peers. Obviously, if a student never engages in "extra" activities at school, he or she will seldom have to deal with the negative actions or comments of others.

We should always encourage adolescents to get involved in numerous activities, clubs, groups, and sports. Also, we must work with them on how to cope with the various "attacks" they may encounter from others. Help provide them with the necessary strategies to handle these tough situations without getting too angry or upset.

Strategy #52

MAKING THE RIGHT MOVES

We need fewer computers and more chess boards in our schools. In his book, *The Flickering Mind*, author Todd Oppenheimer writes, "Since the late 1800's, chess has been proven in study after study to expand players' capacity for concentration, visual memory, quick calculation, logical thinking, problem-solving, and even creativity." (p. 359). From their website *chessintheschools*, it is noted, " Research demonstrates the positive impact of chess on academic performance and emotional intelligence…students who play chess regularly show improved emotional control and mood management, increased patience and persistence."

I have talked with numerous teachers who have used chess to help adolescents gain more control of their emotions, especially anger. In the June 16, 2004 *USA TODAY*, there was an excellent article about a chess teacher in Atlanta named Orrin Hudson. Over the years he has used chess in school to help turn around many tough, inner city kids. Hudson likes to compare the "moves" one makes in chess to the "moves" one makes in life. When it comes to anger, making the wrong move could cause an adolescent to get into serious trouble, but if the adolescent is able to make the right move to control his/her anger, then there is less of a chance of more negative consequences.

Here are some quotes from Hudson that appeared in the newspaper:

- "I teach them, 'Look, you can make one move in life—and never recover. You've got to always ask, 'Is this the best move I can make?' If you see a good move, look for a better move."

- "When you play chess, all your pieces have a clear purpose. Just like in life. You have to make sure you make the right move at the right time."

- "In life, you've got to position yourself to win by coming to school early, by being ready to learn. You've got to make sure you make smart moves. If somebody says, 'Let's not go to school today. Let's play hooky,' you say, 'No; I'm not going to do that. I'm going to make a smart move.'" (p. 4A).

Consider finding time on a weekly basis to let your students play chess. You may also want to consider organizing an after school chess club.

Strategy #53

ANGER AS A MOTIVATOR

We often think of the negative consequences of anger, but anger can also have positive consequences. Anger can actually be a great motivator. For example, when I get angry at all the litter I see along the road, I take action. I may write an editorial in the newspaper or attempt to join an "Adopt a Highway" group. At my school I may get angry because I witness a lot of poor manners in the cafeteria. My anger motivates me to do more classroom lessons on manners.

Adolescents should be encouraged to "use" their anger in positive ways. For example, if Jennifer has concerns about the eighth graders not having enough time to walk the track on a daily basis, instead of complaining, she may set up an appointment with the principal to discuss the matter. She could also bring up the concern at the next Student Council meeting.

Have students complete Skill Sheet #8. It invites them to find positive ways to use their anger. Hopefully they will learn that anger can be a great motivator.

Strategy #54

MORE MORAL STORIES PLEASE

Many educators think that "stories with a moral" are for elementary students only. I disagree. Students at **all** levels need to read and hear stories that emphasize goodness and doing the right thing. Author Robert Coles urges adults to read children stories that stress the development of a moral and spiritual intelligence. Todd Oppenheimer, in his book, *The Flickering Mind*, writes, "Waldorf teachers go even further. They believe that when students go through school without such stories, their ability to develop a sense of empathy is inhibited and that this limits their capacity to find meaning in life." (p. 382). So try your best to fit a few "moral stories" into your weekly lessons.

DON'T GET MAD, GET SMARTER!

Directions: Take a few minutes to think of things that cause you to get angry with your-self, your peers, your family members, and society. Then, think of ways to use that anger to make positive changes in your life. Instead of getting mad, get smarter. Take action!

■ Something about me that gets me angry is _____

_____

■ What positive actions/behaviors can I take to make a change? _____

_____

_____

_____

■ One thing that angers me about one of my peers/classmates is _____

_____

■ Instead of complaining, arguing and getting upset, what are some actions I can take that may change things?

_____

_____

_____

_____

_____

■ An issue that causes me to get angry with a family member is _____

_____

■ What can I do to improve the relationship? _____

_____

_____

_____

_____

■ Something in society that angers me. For example, racism, littering, poverty, teasing, bullying, etc.

_____

_____

■ Now, what are some ways I can use my anger to make positive changes in society? _____

_____

_____

Strategy #55

YOU MEAN IT'S NORMAL TO GET ANGRY ONCE IN A WHILE

In Gregg Easterbrook's book, *The Progress Paradox: How Life Gets Better While People Feel Worse*, he writes, "The preaching of self-esteem, now common in public schools and in the midafternoon-television and talk-radio universe, instills the idea that a person ought always to be beaming with satisfaction, and if not, that he or she must have been wronged by someone or some institution and should be angry. Fixation on self-esteem may, in the end, only cause us to go looking for things to become upset about. People who go looking for things to become upset rarely fail to find them." (p. 184).

Adolescents need to be reminded daily that no one feels good about themselves all the time. Everyone has bad days, setbacks, or periods of time when they feel down, bored, or lousy. Just because Celeste is angry, that doesn't mean there's something wrong with her.

Strategy #56

SET REASONABLE GOALS

Parents and teachers are often guilty of setting unrealistic goals for some adolescents with anger problems. These adults assume that because the teen is no longer in elementary school, he or she should be able to go longer periods of time between outbursts. In elementary school, a teacher might write a plan with second grader Luis that states, "Luis will keep his hands to himself from 8am until 10am." That is a realistic goal for a second grader, but what about an eighth grader? Sure, it would be nice if we could have eighth grade Angel go a whole week without hitting, but her lack of control may be so severe that we have to write a plan similar to the second grader's plan. Once she reaches her goal, we can extend the time frame. Remember, some older students are so volatile that we may have to handle them like we do younger students. If we write plans that are too lengthy or too detailed, we may be setting the student up for failure.

Strategy #57

AVOID THE "IT'S JUST EASIER" SYNDROME

I'm seeing a distressing syndrome occurring in our country that I call, "It's just easier." When it comes to their adolescents, many parents are guilty of saying things like:

- Oh, it's just easier to let him hang out in the neighborhood. I don't have the time or energy to check up on him.

- Oh, it's just easier to let him listen to that nasty music. I'm done nagging him.

- Oh, it's just easier to let her dress like that. I'm done arguing with her.

- I'm so busy I don't have time to do a "background check" on every boy she goes out with. It's just easier for me to let her use her own judgment.

Teachers and parents must do all they can to avoid this syndrome. Adolescents, even though they may not admit it, want and need our guidance. Set rules and limits. Be consistent. Parenting and teaching these youngsters takes much time and energy.

Strategy #58

COSTLY INSULTS

Adolescents are good at tossing insults at each other. Recipients of the insults usually react in three different ways. Some can ignore the rudeness while others withdraw and cry. Then there are those who get very angry. Obviously I encourage students not to return insults and I also remind them that when they do ignore, they are showing maturity and self-control. Following is an ancient tale that I love to read to young people. The story helps them to see the wisdom in ignoring insults. The story comes from Tom Merton's book, *The Wisdom of the Desert*.

Once there was a disciple of a Greek philosopher who was commanded by his Master for three years to give money to everyone who insulted him. When this period was over, the Master said to him: Now you can go to Athens and learn wisdom. When the disciple was entering Athens he met a certain wise man who sat at the gate insulting everybody who came and went. He also insulted the disciple who immediately burst out laughing. Why do you laugh when I insult you? said the wise man. Because, said the disciple, for three years I have been paying for this kind of thing and now you give it to me for nothing. Enter the city, said the wise man, it is all yours.

(p. 39)

Strategy #59

GRATITUDE JOURNALING

Gratitude research is beginning to suggest that feelings of thankfulness have tremendous positive value in helping people cope with daily problems, especially stress, and to achieve a positive sense of the self.
— Robert Emmons
University of California at Davis

Unhappy people tend to focus on all the negative things that happen. They seldom take the time to appreciate nature, peace, supportive parents, having enough to eat, or a nice roof over their heads. These people may benefit from keeping a "gratitude journal" in which they note things in their lives for which they are thankful. In his book, *The Progress Paradox*, Gregg Easterbrook notes, "In an experiment with college students, those who kept a gratitude journal, a weekly record of things they feel grateful for, achieved better physical health, were more optimistic, exercised more regularly, and described themselves as happier than a control group of students who kept no journals but had the same overall measures of health, optimism, and exercise when the experiment began." (p. 239).

Skill Sheet #9 is a sample page of a gratitude journal. Make copies for your students and have them keep a weekly record.

GRATITUDE JOURNAL

- Date: _____
- Things for which I am grateful _____
_____
_____
_____

- Date: _____
- Things for which I am grateful _____
_____
_____
_____

- Date: _____
- Things for which I am grateful _____
_____
_____
_____

- Date: _____
- Things for which I am grateful _____
_____
_____
_____

- Date: _____
- Things for which I am grateful _____
_____
_____
_____

Strategy #60

TIME IN VS. TIME OUT

When working with adolescents, try to avoid using the term "timeout." They see this term as childish; only little kids are sent to timeout. Instead, think in terms of "time in."

- Lucinda, you need a few minutes of "time in" quiet thought.
- Hank, please take five minutes of "time in" the breathing room.
- Jermaine, you could use ten minutes of "time in" vigorous exercise.

Strategy #61

TURNING DISAPPOINTMENTS INTO APPOINTMENTS

It usually doesn't take much to upset or anger an adolescent. Things like not getting invited to a party, not making the team, failing a quiz, or losing a boy/girl friend can be major disappointments. I encourage people to turn their disappointments into appointments. When things go wrong they need to schedule an appointment with themselves and answer the following questions.

- What did I learn from this setback?
- Could it have been worse?
- Was it really that big of a deal?
- Could I have handled things differently?
- When I'm feeling down, what positive thing can I do for myself or others?

Also, remind young people that quite often when bad things happen, good things follow. Think of a time in your life when things didn't work out the way you wished and you were very angry. Then later on some good things came out of your disappointment. Share a personal story with the students.

Strategy #62

SENDING OUT INVITATIONS

Over the years I worked with many extremely challenging students who had anger and behavior problems. One successful strategy I've used is to get these students involved in some type of physical activity that allows them to burn off their anger in a positive way. Every year at my school I head up a wrestling club for students in grades 3-5. Many of the boys who join the club have behavior and anger problems. The yearly clubs go on for two weeks. I have seen dramatic improvement in many of the participants. I truly believe that I've done more to help some of these kids in two weeks of wrestling than I could in twenty counseling sessions!

Many angry/challenging adolescents will not willingly sign up for sports on their own, but I have noticed something remarkable that happens when they are sent invitations to join. If you notice that a student has a special gift or talent, notify the coach and ask him or her to invite the student to join. Many do. My son coaches wrestling at a middle school. He is constantly seeking out boys who could benefit from his program. He meets individually with these students and encourages them to join. Every year he has an abundance of wrestlers!

48

Strategy #63

BE A TRAIL ANGEL

For most runners, myself included, the ultimate experience would be to complete the Boston Marathon. For hikers, it would probably be covering all 2,174 miles of the Appalachian Trail that runs from Springer Mountain in Georgia to Mount Katahdin, Maine. Hikers on that long, torturous trail face numerous adversities such as dehydration, lack of sleep, encounters with bears, snakebites, not enough to eat, cold weather, sunburn, illness, nasty mosquitoes, and fatigue. All along the trail live kind people known as Trail Angels. Their goal is to assist hikers in different ways. Some Trail Angels leave water on the path. Some pass out warm pastries while others invite hikers in to their homes for dinner and a hot shower. Trail Angels give tired hikers a ride to town and leave candy and Cokes at overnight shelters. Most hikers never see these special, caring people. The Trail Angels do not have to do these generous things, but their actions help hikers reach their goal of finishing the long trek.

Angry adolescents also face numerous adversities on their daily travels: teasing, bullying, uncaring adults, academic failures, peers encouraging them to smoke, drink alcohol, pressure from gang members, and family problems. These needy adolescents could benefit from Trail Angels in their lives. Consider being one. Do a few special and secretive good deeds daily for young people who are struggling. Your "gifts" could help some of these students have a better day and prevent possible outbursts.

Here are a few Trail Angel activities.

- Find out what kind of candy bar Lenny likes. Secretly place one on his desk once in a while.

- If Kenny is getting nervous, offer him a piece of gum.

- When Ben leaves your room to go to a teacher whom he doesn't getting along with very well with, offer a few words of encouragement.

- Write a positive note to Jasmine, and hide it in her book bag.

- Strike up a conversation with Maurice as he walks by the group of boys who usually tease him.

- Say something positive about Lillie to a teacher who has problems with her in a different class.

Strategy #64

PERSONAL MANTRAS

When we think of mantras we often think about monks high on a mountain top chanting for hours. Most of us don't have the time during the busy school day to do much chanting, but I do think it is not a bad idea to have a personal mantra to repeat to ourselves on a regular basis. Our personal mantras may help us to control our emotions when dealing with difficult adolescents. One of the funniest episodes of the television show *Sienfeld* centered around George's father who was working on his anger. A therapist encouraged George's father to shout out "Serenity Now!" whenever he started to get upset. I'm not suggesting you shout out "Serenity Now" in front of your class, but you could repeat your mantras before going to work in the morning or you could repeat them quietly to yourself before responding to a hostile student.

I have a personal mantra that I use on a regular basis. It goes, "All days are good, but some are better than others." In his book, *Taking Charge of Anger*, W. Robert Nay suggests that we consider the following mantra when the chips are down.

> *I am powerless over everyone but myself. What they say, do, think, and feel is their right as long as it doesn't hurt others. It is not my job to be a parent, teacher, police officer, spiritual leader, or critic; that takes time and robs me of my energy. I can focus on problem solving by how I decide to react to what they do or just accept what I cannot change. Either way, I can be calm. Either way, they will continue to do what they choose to do. (p.66)*

Strategy #65

TO CHEW OR NOT TO CHEW

Anger is energy. One way to burn off that energy is to chew gum. I always keep sugarless gum handy and offer a piece to people who seem to be getting angry. Besides burning off anger, there are many more positive benefits of gum chewing. Following is a list of a dozen reasons why we should consider allowing students to chew gum.

A DOZEN REASONS FOR LETTING THEM CHEW

> *As of this day, this hour, this second, there will be no more gum chewing allowed in this class without teacher permission. Frequent violators will receive negative consequences.*
>
> — Written on the blackboard in a middle school classroom

To chew or not to chew, that is the question.

Educators have been debating the gum chewing issue for many, many years. In some classrooms students are free to chew away while in other classrooms it is a serious violation. Teachers have been known to have violators write, "I will not chew gum in class" five hundred times. A few principals have sentenced students to ten days in in-school suspension for packing some Wrigley's in their book bags. I personally know two janitors who would chase gum chewers down the hall with a broom stick!

Strategy #65

TO CHEW OR NOT TO CHEW

(continued)

I must confess, I am a school gum chewer and I think it's time I took a stand for others who like to pop a stick of Bazooka or Juicy Fruit while reading a book or trying to solve a tricky math problem. I've worked in schools for twenty-five years, counseled hundreds of students, written several books on discipline, and presented hundreds of workshops for classroom teachers. All of this experience, plus hours of research, has led me to this conclusion: Gum chewing offers several benefits to students.

What's so great about gum chewing?

- **It helps keep teeth clean.** Dentists have reported that chewing sugarless gum stimulates saliva, which helps to clean teeth.

- **It helps adolescents control anger.** It doesn't take much for a teenager to get angry. Anger is energy. Many vent their anger in negative ways such as hitting, pushing, name-calling, and breaking things. They need alternative ways of releasing their anger/energy. Chewing gum is one activity. Chewing hard and fast can help defuse an angry adolescent.

- **It assists those with anxieties.** Just like anger, nervousness produces energy. Young people turn that nervous energy into sweating, nail-biting, pulling hair, tapping on a desk, or other behaviors. A stick of gum may help calm the child and give him an outlet to burn off the energy. Then he may be better prepared to take that tough test or to speak in front of his peers.

- **It helps with concentration.** Have you ever watched a baseball game on television? Did you notice that almost every player is chewing something? More and more players today are not chewing tobacco, they are chewing gum. Baseball is a game that demands a great deal of concentration. If baseball players chew to help with concentration, then why wouldn't chewing help students to do a better job of paying attention? In the February 2, 2004 issue of *The New Yorker*, Ben McGrath tells of an experiment that Dr. Kenneth Allen did with some of his students at N.Y.U.'s College of Dentistry. In his CD-ROM experiment, half of the students were allowed to chew gum while studying, and half were not allowed to chew. After three days of instruction (in person and via CD, gummed and gumless), the students were tested. To his surprise, the gum chewers scored, on average, a B-minus on the written component while abstainers managed only a C-plus. Did the chewing help them concentrate better and, in turn, get them a higher grade? Food for thought!

- **It can help with acid reflux and heartburn symptoms.** A recent study at Kings College in London found that chewing gum for 30 minutes after a potentially troublesome fatty meal can reduce acid exposure in the esophagus and help reduce heartburn symptoms. We know that many young people eat too much fat, so let them chew after lunch. It may help keep them in class instead of the nurse's office.

- **It helps cover up bad breath.** Do I need to say anything more about this benefit?

- **It can be used as a tool for teaching manners.** Students need to learn how to chew properly (not loudly, no cracking sounds, and no blowing bubbles in class). Their chewing should not become annoying to others. Also, they need to know where and where not to chew. No gum in the media center or computer lab. No chewing during the Pledge of Allegiance or the National Anthem. In the August 9, 2004 issue of *Sports Illustrated*, there was a report about Russian president Vladmir Putin who scolded his country's national soccer team because he saw them chewing gum during the Russian national anthem.

- **It helps smokers battle nicotine withdrawals.** Unfortunately, many of our teens are addicted to cigarettes. It is very difficult for them to go long periods of time without a puff. By letting Cindy chew gum, she might make it through third period instead of skipping class and heading to the bushes for a smoke.

- **It is a good substitute for junk food.** Wouldn't you rather see Jacob chewing sugarless gum than gulping down a 3 Musketeers candy bar?

- **It helps make the brain work better.** A recent study at the University of Northumbria in England found, "Chewing gum may help make people smarter by improving memory and brain performance. In tests, scientists found the ability to recall remembered words improved by 35% among people who chewed." The researchers think the improved performance is based on the belief that chewing raises the heart beat, which causes more oxygen and nutrients to be pumped into the brain.

- **It helps increase weight-loss.** In an August, 2004 issue of *The New England Journal of Medicine*, there was an interesting article about research done at the Mayo Clinic in Rochester, Minnesota. The researchers noted that if a person chewed a piece of sugarless gum, at 100 chews per minute, all day long, every day, all year-long, he would lose eleven pounds!

- **It can help teach responsibility.** Chewing gum should be considered a privilege. Those who do not follow class rules about gum chewing need to lose the privilege for a period of time. I don't think the whole class should be punished because Lenny left his wad on the floor. A possible consequence for violations may involve helping the janitor do some cleaning. I've encouraged teachers to attach small "gum buckets" to each desk. When students are finished chewing, they can toss their gum in the little buckets. Have students take turns emptying the buckets. I believe students who are allowed to chew, and who are provided with a place to discard gum, are less likely to be sneaky and stick it up under their desk tops.

Let's not become another Singapore!

I hope this strategy has helped you "rethink" your student gum chewing philosophy. Give the students a chance to show they can be responsible. They may concentrate better, lose weight, be less angry, and be smarter!

The country of Singapore just lifted its notorious ban on chewing gum after 12 years. That's right; gum chewing was illegal because a former leader thought it fouled streets, buildings, buses and subway trains. People were actually jailed for violating the gum law. Let's not be like the old Singapore. Let's be like the new Singapore. If that country is willing to give gum chewing another try, so should we.

CATEGORY 3:
STRONG ANGER

Strategy #66

THE "D" ESCALATOR

Here is a clever four-step tool for students to use when they begin to get angry. It is adapted from a workshop presented by The Applebaum Training Institute in Sugar Land, Texas.

A... Arrest yourself

B... Breathe

C... Compliment yourself

D... Deeply breathe again

Strategy #67

GET ON YOUR HORSE PAUL REVERE

Do you remember the American history lesson about Paul Revere riding his horse through town shouting, "The British are coming! The British are coming!"? Obviously he was warning people of potential danger. If you work with a violent, explosive student, you need to find out what the triggers are. Once you do, then you may need to "get on your horse" and inform others on the staff. For example, if Rex doesn't like to be teased about his red hair, then other staff members need to be aware of it. Also, other students should be encouraged to avoid comments about his hair. The more people who are aware of this, the fewer outbursts there should be.

Strategy #68

FALSE ACCUSATIONS

Have you ever accused a student of doing something wrong, only to find out later you made a mistake? How did you feel? Did you apologize to the student? How did the student react to your false accusation? How did the student accept your apology?

Quite often teens get blamed for things they didn't do. Have you ever tried to put yourself in their shoes and think about how they feel? Can you understand why they might get angry? Here's a chance for adolescents to express their feelings about false accusations. Have them complete Skill Sheet #10: **False Accusations**. Follow up this activity with a class discussion.

Strategy #69

THE MORE STEPS, THE MERRIER

When we think of elementary school children we think of playtime and how important it is for youngsters to get outside, but what about older students? Don't they need play, movement, and exercise on a regular basis? I know that schedules at middle and high school are tight and sometimes it is difficult to "spare" a few minutes for walking and/or running. According to a recent study at California State University, it may benefit teachers and students if we can find the time to get everyone up and moving. In the December, 2003 issue of *Spirituality & Health*, Dr. Robert Thayer conducted a study in which he had participants wear pedometers, devices that count the steps they took for ten days. They kept a record of their daily moods. As it turned out, the more steps they walked each day, the higher their energy level and the better they felt. They were happier and had less tension and stress.

Adolescents need time to exercise and socialize. Maybe you can combine both by finding time for them to walk the track with their friends. It wouldn't hurt for us to join them. Adults need the fresh air and exercise just as much as the students do.

FALSE ACCUSATIONS

Directions: Read the following newspaper article from the June 29, 2004 issue of *The Kansas City Star*. Then answer the questions. Follow up with a class discussion.

TEENS TAKE THE BLAME FOR SQUIRREL'S THEFT

Bettendorf, Iowa. A couple has finally discovered what was happening to the yellow ribbons they were tying to the trees in their yard in support of their son and other troops in Iraq. "The ribbons started to disappear. Every time it disappeared, I would hang a new one," said Bob Saskowski, who tied the ribbons with his wife, Alexis. It went on for eight months. The last straw was when three ribbons disappeared in three days. So Bob Saskowski appealed to his neighbors through a memo, asking them to talk to their teenagers about respect and patriotism and asked for their help. "It indicated I needed their eyes to help watch the trees," he said. "My husband and I were ticked," said neighbor Patty Kenyon. "And we all decided if this person was going to pick on Bob, then they can pick on all of us. And we literally put ribbons up and down the street." The ribbons kept disappearing, but only from the Saskowski yard.

Finally, the couple set up a video camera, focused on the yard. Six weeks later they caught the culprit on tape. The ribbon was being shimmied slowly down the trunk. At the base, the squirrel pushing the ribbon, bit through the ribbon and took off with it. "We can laugh now," Saskowski said, "Before, it was not funny." He says the squirrel was actually a good thing. "And I named him Patriot because he brought our neighborhood together," Saskowski said.

- Have you ever been blamed or accused of something you didn't do? _____

- How did it make you feel? _____

- Do you think that many teens get falsely accused of things they didn't do? _____

- Most of the time, do the teachers and parents apologize? _____

- What was your reaction to the above newspaper article? _____
_____
_____
_____

- In the article, why do think the Saskowskis thought teens were taking the ribbons? _____
_____
_____
_____

Strategy #70

TEMPERAMENTS DETERMINE PEER GROUPS

Have you ever noticed how a person's temperament determines his or her peer group? People tend to congregate with others who have similar behaviors/personalities. If you don't believe that temperament determines peer groups, take a close look at your next faculty meeting! Heaven forbid you have any negative teachers at your school, but if you do, you'll notice that they sit together. I don't enjoy sitting next to negative, complaining people, so I look to sit next to other faculty members like me who enjoy jokes, playing tricks, and acting silly.

Students are no different from us. Closely study your students. Do the shy kids hang out with the bullies? No! Do the impulsive, risk-takers hang out with other impulsive, risk-takers? Yes! If you have any angry, moody, temperamental students, try to get them matched up and involved with other students who are more calm, patience, and easy-going. Keep angry students apart; they often "feed" off each other.

Here are a couple of my favorite quotes about the influence of peers. You may wish to post them in your classroom.

"The friends you keep, determines the trouble you meet."

— anonymous

"The next best thing to being wise is to live in a circle of those who are."

— C. S. Lewis

Strategy #71

SOLITUDE: Rx FOR THE ATTITUDE

Elementary teachers often send students to "time out" when they need time to calm down and think about their behaviors. We usually don't think of utilizing time outs with middle and high school students, but often these older students do need a location to go where they can get their emotions under control. A few minutes of quiet and solitude can do wonders. I often seek time alone when I begin to get overly stressed. How about you? When and where do you find solitude?

Strategy #72

EMPATHETIC ASSERTION

Yes, when confronting an angry adolescent, we may get better results if we show some empathy before seeking a resolution. The term "empathic assertion" refers to the process of acknowledging the angry person's feelings before confronting the issues. For instance, tenth-grader Olivia rushes into math class just as the bell rings. The teacher can see that Olivia is angry and asks, "What's wrong?" She replies, "I just saw my boyfriend kissing another girl!" Olivia starts to mumble and disrupts class.

Now, what do you think is more important to Olivia at this time.....math or the fact that her boyfriend is cheating on her? Following are two responses the teacher could use. The first one may add fuel to the fire. The second response includes empathic assertion which should help to defuse the situation.

- **Response #1:** "Olivia, this is math class! You leave your boyfriend problems out of here. Now settle down and get to work!"

- **Response #2:** (Empathic assertion) "Olivia, I'm sorry about the boyfriend problem. Try to settle down, take a few deep breaths, and I won't call on you for a while. I don't blame you for being angry. Maybe you can work on this issue later."

Strategy #73

YES, YOU COULD HAVE DONE BETTER

In the past when I encountered an angry student I would often say something like, "Justin, you could have done worse. At least you didn't break anything or hit anyone." Recently I've started to "rethink" that approach. By saying, "Justin, you could have done worse," may not be as effective as saying, "Justin, you could have done better." By using the latter statement, it places more responsibility back on Justin to practice the skills I taught him to control his anger. Justin's goal should be to "do better" when utilizing anger management skills. Compare these statements to an English teacher who discusses Justin's grade of C on a report. The teacher would likely say to Justin, "You could have done better" instead of, "You could have done worse." Just like in the academic setting, we should be encouraging the Justins of the world to strive for excellence by always "doing better."

Strategy #74

THE DRINKERS OF THE WIND

I am a serious runner. During the past twenty-three years I've run over 31,000 miles and completed seven marathons. Running helps me stay in shape and keeps my weight down. One of the other benefits of my running is its affect on my temperament. It calms me, lowers my frustration level, and is an excellent outlet for venting any anger that enters my body. Running has changed my life in many ways.

When I work with counselors and teachers I encourage them set up running programs at their school for all students, not just the angry ones! The best time to have the students run is first thing in the morning. The running burns off excess energy and actually calms the students, which helps them to behave better. The running also sends oxygen to the brain which enhances academic performance.

If you set up a running program at your school, be sure to give the group a name and allow each member to earn a t-shirt. Of all the clubs I've heard about, my favorite one was called, *The Drinkers of the Wind*.

Strategy #75

THE HARD-HEARTED

Angry people are often labeled, "hard-hearted." Sometimes we feel that if we could just "soften" their hearts, they wouldn't be so angry. The word *heart* is used regularly in our everyday language, not solely in reference to anger. Have your students form small groups of three or four and complete Skill Sheet #11. They'll enjoy discovering and understanding the numerous ways the word heart is used in today's language.

HEART EXPRESSIONS

Directions: There is an ancient belief that the heart was literally the seat of emotion, intellect, and memory. Many people today still possess this belief. Almost daily you hear the heart expressions below. As a group, try to discover the meaning of these expressions. Give it your best shot before asking adults for help.

❤ Heart of gold _____

❤ Hard-hearted _____

❤ Heart on a sleeve _____

❤ Heart's in the right place _____

❤ Heart-to-heart talk _____

❤ Learn by heart _____

❤ Heart of stone _____

❤ Heavy heart _____

❤ Have a heart! _____

Strategy #76

LOAD UP THE BUS FOR A HEART TOUR

All of us today could do a better job of showing more compassion for others. We need to explore our hearts daily. Adolescents are often guilty of not showing compassion and they can become self-centered, cold, and even hostile to those who are different. Seldom do they take the time to examine their hearts. This strategy offers teachers a unique approach for working with these self-centered students. It involves taking students on Heart Tours. A Heart Tour is a three step program.

■ **Step 1:** Teacher selects a group of people to study and students are asked to talk about their feelings concerning this group. For instance, the teacher opens a discussion about homeless people. Students are encouraged to explore their hearts and express honest feelings about the homeless. The teacher should not give his or her opinion at this time. Students should feel free to state their true feelings.

■ **Step 2:** Teacher arranges a bus trip to the city to observe the homeless. Students are encouraged to take notes and, if allowed, interview a few of them.

■ **Step 3:** On the following day the teacher asks the students to take another tour of their heart. The teacher may ask questions such as: Have your thoughts/opinions changed after the trip to the city? Are you more compassionate now? Are all the homeless lazy? Why are some people homeless? How do they survive, eat, and stay warm? Could you survive long on the streets? Do you plan on doing anything to help the homeless?

Skill Sheet #12 provides you with an outline to use on your Heart Tours.

Strategy #77

A THERMOS OF CHAMOMILE

For centuries people have discovered numerous beneficial uses of herbal teas. Chamomile is one such herbal tea that is often used to help calm and relax people. Why not let students with anger problems keep some in a container and let them have a swallow or two several times during the day, especially during stressful moments? Oh, by the way, don't let them drink too much because they might fall asleep!

HEART TOUR FORM

Directions: This form should be distributed to each student before the actual bus trip. Students are encouraged to keep all these forms in a notebook so they can revisit them often to note changes in their thoughts/opinions.

STEP #1:

■ Who or what is to be studied/explored? *(i.e., homeless, prisoners, police officers, endangered animals, polluted rivers, etc).* _____

■ Today's date: _____

■ Take a tour of your heart. What are your thoughts, feelings, opinions, likes and dislikes on this subject or group of people? Be honest! _____
_____
_____
_____
_____

STEP #2:

■ Date of tour. _____

■ Location of tour. Where did you visit? _____

■ What did you observe? _____
_____
_____

■ Other notes and bits of information. _____
_____
_____
_____
_____
_____

STEP #3:

■ Today's date: _____

■ Likes and dislikes about the tour _____
_____
_____
_____

■ What did you learn? _____
_____
_____

■ Take another tour of your heart. Have your thoughts and opinions changed since before the bus tour? ___
How? _____
_____
_____

Strategy #78

MAKING DEPOSITS FOR THE NEEDY

Here is an interesting concept to ponder. I read about a man who would always put a dollar in a jar when he got angry. When his jar was full, he would donate it to charity. Soon he realized that getting angry was expensive. After a while he began to do a better job of controlling his anger but missed the good feeling of giving his money to the homeless shelter. So he decided to change his game plan. He started putting a dollar in the jar every time he **was** able to control himself, and, of course, he gave that money to charity.

Get creative. Maybe you can think of various ways to use this idea with an individual adolescent or with the whole class. Instead of money, you might consider using tokens. As the individual, or the class as a whole improves, drop tokens in a jar. Once the jar is full, do something to help the needy.

Strategy #79

ENJOYING THE ATTENTION

At times it appears that students enjoy being angry because they get so much attention. I've witnessed middle school students getting upset and have peers flocked around them to find out why they are angry. I've heard students say to their angry peers, "Why are you mad?" "What's wrong?" "Talk to me." "Did I do something to upset you?" Occasionally a student will purposely display his/her anger for long periods of time just to get attention.

It is appropriate for an adult to ask, "What's wrong?" or "What can I do to help you?" After your initial inquiries, back away. Do not continue to interrogate the adolescent. Don't give the student any more attention at that time. If you have developed a trusting relationship with the student, eventually he or she will share concerns.

Strategy #80

DANGEROUS E-MAILS

Today's adolescents are hooked on instant messages. They are quick to send off a reply on their computers, but this form of communication can be dangerous to an angry boy or girl. I suggest to my students that they respond to the person they are upset with by writing a letter. Writing takes more time than sending an e-mail. This allows the adolescent to calm down and do more thinking as they write a response. Because sending e-messages are quick and easy, some young people send off a reply when they are very angry. They may end up regretting it, especially if they say some hurtful things. Also, the recipient of the "hot" message may copy it to show others. DON'T SEND E-MESSAGES WHEN ANGRY!

Strategy #81

DEFEATED BY THE POWER RANGERS

Every school has a small number of students who get on their "high horses" and travel throughout the campus, teasing and bullying others. They also like to gossip and spread rumors. Their actions can be hurtful and cause many innocent students to get angry. I call these unkind students, Power Rangers. Even after they leave the scene of the crime, their power continues to affect the targeted victim. For example, Power Ranger Janice laughs at Julie and her "dollar store" dress, then rides away. A few minutes later when Janice is on the other side of campus, Julie is still upset. Janice is nowhere around, but her power is still eating at Julie. I tell victims not to be defeated by the Power Rangers. They must do all they can to shrug it off and go on their why. They should not give their rude peers the pleasure of knowing they have ruined their day. In middle school I often reminded students, "Don't get defeated by the Power Rangers!"

Strategy #82

STOP, THINK, THEN ACT

So many angry adolescents are guilty of "reacting" without thinking. Then, later on they feel ashamed or remorseful. Somehow we have to get them to slow down, be patient, and think before taking action. Have your students complete Skill Sheet #13. The story is based on a true event. Hopefully the story and activity will make them think.

TICKETS, TIRES, & TEENS

Directions: Read the story and answer the questions.

Heavy snow was falling outside a small diner just north of Lewiston, Montana. It was dark and freezing as Jamie and Conrad stuck out their thumbs, hoping for a ride to Chinook. The two teenagers were getting extremely frustrated because no cars stopped. Soon they started swearing and giving the "middle finger" at those who whizzed by. Around nine o'clock a small Volkswagen bug pulled into the diner parking lot. An older gentleman got out and headed inside for a coffee. His little car was packed full of boxes, books, clothes, and suitcases. The teens approached the man and asked, "Hey, are you traveling north?" The man said he was. Jamie responded, "Hey can you give us a lift to Chinook?" The man replied, "I'm sorry. I don't have enough room for two more people in my little car. Plus, I'm stopping off to pick up a friend. He'll be sitting up front with me."

Conrad said to Jamie, "He could have given us a ride!" Jamie said, "What are we going to do? We don't have any money. It's getting late. It's snowing hard and there aren't going to be any more cars on the road in a while." Conrad responded, "I'm sick and tired of people not helping us! Give me your pen knife." Jamie asked, "Conrad, what are you going to do?" Conrad took the thin knife and poked a small hole in each tire on the Volkswagen. Then he mumbled, "That will teach the old man! By the time he gets a few miles out of town his tires will be flat and he'll be in the middle of nowhere freezing. That'll teach him not to help us!"

They continued to hitch hike as the man came out of the diner. The man handed the boys a small brown bag and then drove away as air leaked out of his four tires. Jamie asked Conrad, "What's in the bag?" Conrad reached into the bag and pulled out a roll of money and a small note. The note read:

> *I'm sorry I couldn't give you guys a ride. I didn't have enough room. I was worried about you being cold and far from home so I told everyone in the diner about your dilemma. I passed this bag around and almost everybody tossed in a few dollars to help you. Here is enough money to go across the street to the bus station and purchase two tickets to Chinook.*
>
> *God bless the both of you,*
> *Pastor Kris Sanders*

- How do think the boys felt as they saw the man drive away with air leaking from his tires? _____
  _____

- Did they over react? _____
  _____

- How do you think the boys felt when they found out he was a pastor? _____
  _____

- Do you think the boys will change? Will they be more patient and kinder to others? _____
  _____

Strategy #83

WHEN "WE" GET ANGRY

Although this book focuses on adolescents with anger problems, the adults who read it can get angry at times. Students have a way of "ruffling our feathers." Because of their actions, we have to give consequences, but I hope parents and teachers calm down before shouting out those consequences. I have the following quote posted on my desk as a reminder.

Let Your Emotions Subside Before You Decide.

Strategy #84

MEDITATION IMPACTS TEEN BLOOD PRESSURE

A 2003 study by the Medical College of Georgia found that two 15-minute meditation sessions each day—once at home, the other at school—helped teenage students lower their blood pressure over four months. Their blood pressure even continued to drop for four months after the meditation sessions ended. Researchers screened 5,000 students and found 156 with high blood pressure. Half of the 156 teens received meditation sessions and the other half, a control group, did not. All the students wore blood pressure monitors 24 hours a day. The control group did not have any reduction in blood pressure.

Many of today's teens are extremely busy and prone to stress, anger, frustration and increased blood pressure. Vernon Barnes, a physiologist at the medical school, encourages educators to include time for meditation during the school day to help these students. Counselors may devise plans with targeted students that include a mediation session before school begins in the morning and another session at home later in the day.

Strategy #85

THE MORE MUSCLE, THE MORE MEMORY

Many of us can remember when we were seniors in high school and had to write a term paper in order to graduate. I remember it well. There were no computers with spell-check, no Internet, and no "Google.com." I had to choose a topic, go to the library to search the card catalog, find the books, hand write notes, do an outline, and then use the typewriter. It took much time and energy to finish. Now days, students sit in front of a computer and complete research papers in minutes without burning off many calories. There's an old saying that says, "The more muscle, the more memory." The more energy, movement, and "hands on" experience students have, the more they learn. Most educators agree that students learn best by doing, not sitting and listening.

Let's take the "more muscle, more memory" theory one step further. If this approach helps students learn more, could it help some students to behave better? For example, Jason is a high-energy, easily-distracted, and oftentimes, angry eighth grader. Instead of having him sit through a 40-minute lecture on Native American history, could the teacher give him material to build a teepee or construct a smoke house? My experience finds that a limited amount of movement helps many students to learn more and behave better.

Strategy #86

ADOLESCENT ANGER RATING SCALE

One of the best instruments for determining anger issues in young people is the Adolescent Anger Rating Scale. The purpose of this scale is to assess the various levels and types of adolescent responses to anger. It is appropriate for ages 11-19 and takes only a few minutes to administer. It can be given individually or in groups. The AARS is a 41-item psychometrically sound instrument that assess the intensity and frequency of anger expression. The items are consistent with behaviors identified in the DSM –IV. Elevated scores can help to identify adolescents who are at risk for diagnosis of Conduct Disorder, Oppositional Defiant Disorder, and ADHD.

For more information and to order, contact Psychological Assessment Resources in Lutz, FL.

Strategy #87

GOING WEST BY SAILING EAST

First of all we need a quick geography lesson. We all know that if we are in Nevada and wish to go to California, we need to go west but, isn't it possible to eventually get to California by going east? It may take a lot longer, but we would get there! Now let's relate this geography lesson to dealing with anger. Here is a personal example. Let's say I'm walking up the hall in school and "overhear" Ms. Wallace say something very untrue about one of my difficult students. When I hear it I get very angry. Instead of going directly to her and confronting her when my emotions are high, I decide to go the long way around to get to her. I'll walk slowly all around the building to get back to her. By doing this I've burned off some energy, calmed down, and had time to think. When I was upset with her, I sailed west in order to go east!

Teach your impulsive, quick-tempered adolescents to avoid going directly towards the person they are upset with. Encourage them to take the long route. They can walk around the halls, take a few laps on the track, or even go cool-off in the bathroom for a few minutes.

Strategy #88

THE GRIZZLY BEAR GROWL

Some "anger experts" encourage people to scream out loud as a way of defusing their anger. I personally don't suggest screaming. I offer my clients the Grizzly Bear Growl as an alternative to screaming. I've been known to use it myself quite often and when I finish I usually feel much better! Here is how it works. Go in your room, office, or head outside. Get up on your toes; raise your hands high with fingers bent like claws. Just like a disturbed grizzly bear, try to make yourself as big as possible. Then let out a long, loud growl. Try to let the growl go on for five to ten seconds. Try it. I guarantee much of your anger will fizzle and you'll feel much better. After you have mastered this unique and fantastic trick, teach it to your students. If you do, then be aware, some days your class may sound like a zoo!

Strategy #89

ARE YOU 100% SURE?

Make a large sign that reads "Are you 100% sure?" See Skill Sheet #14. Post it on the wall so everyone, including you, can see it. Easily-angered students are often guilty of accusing or blaming others without gathering all the facts. Many times I've heard students say, "He stole my pencil." Then, a few minutes later they find their pencils on the floor or hidden under a book. In middle school, I've seen students get so angry that they wanted to hit someone or something because of "alleged" comments from their peers.

Whenever a student comes to you to blame or accuse others, point to the sign. Also, before you "jump to conclusions" about a student or situation, be sure you look at the sign. Are you 100% sure?

Strategy #90

CONSIDER YOGA

Not long ago a Texas judge created a bit of sensation when he sentenced a man who slapped his wife to take yoga classes as part of his one-year probation. The judge thought the yoga classes would help him control his anger. All across the country people like this judge and others are discovering the benefits of yoga. Every year more schools are implementing yoga programs to help adolescents improve health, concentration, and anger control. Teachers, counselors, and administrators should take a few minutes to learn creative ways schools are using yoga. Yoga classes can be extremely beneficial to adolescents with anger problems. Check out Skill Sheet #15. Make copies and share with other professionals who work with angry adolescents.

Are You 100% Sure?

HOW YOGA HELPS ADOLESCENTS CONTROL ANGER

by Jamie Allison

■ Yoga is experiential.

Literature on working with children with emotional difficulties such as anger often refers to changing negative thoughts or slowing down enough to control angry or reactive responses to situations. Standard "talking" therapies can fall short with some individuals because they have trouble generalizing what they learn in sessions with a counselor or psychologist to real world situations. The individual may know the information but has not had a chance to experience *feeling* a different way. Yoga can give adolescents a chance to experience how it *feels* to be relaxed both in the body and the mind.

■ Yoga calms the nervous system.

Yoga works to allow individuals to feel relaxation by directly impacting the nervous system, moving it from the sympathetic or "crisis" mode to the parasympathetic or "real" mode. Research has shown that participation in even one yoga class can temporarily diminish cortisol (a chemical released during times of stress) levels ("Yoga: An Ancient Practice," Sept/Oct 2003).

■ Yoga releases tension in the body.

Anger automatically makes the body tense and tight. Over time, holding of tension becomes a chronic pattern that an individual may no longer even notice. Yoga poses can involve stretching of muscles, but also opening and release on a deeper level. For example, some poses involve twisting massage and move the internal organs. This can improve blood flow and impact bodily functions such as digestion (Iyenger, 1966). Breathing practices also provide movement for internal organs like the heart, spleen, stomach, and intestines as the diaphragm rises and falls. Even these subtle internal shifts can break up and release tension and held stress. (Farhl, 1996).

■ Yoga can be empowering.

Adolescents dealing with anger sometimes have little real control over difficult family or environmental situations. However, practicing yoga can give individuals a sense of empowerment with what they really *can* control—themselves. They may make noticeable physical gains related to balance, strength, or flexibility. They can learn that they have control over getting to a relaxed place in body and mind. They can learn how to be more aware of their physical, mental, and emotional states, and can then learn to tap into this when they need it. They can develop confidence about what they can do to help themselves.

*Farhl, D. (1996). *The Breathing Book*. New York: Henry Holt and Company.

*Iyengar, B.K.S. (1966). *Light on Yoga*. New York: Schoken Books.

*Yoga: An Ancient Practice for Modern Ills. (Sept/Oct 2003), ACE Fitness Matters, p.5.

Jamie Allison is a school psychologist for Orange County Schools in Hillsborough, North Carolina.

CATEGORY 4:
VERY STRONG ANGER

Strategy #91

SAVE THE MORE INTENSIVE WORK FOR LATER IN THE DAY

Many of our angry adolescents can be dealing with mood disorders, Oppositional Defiant Disorder, or Conduct Disorder. Teachers who have been successful with these challenging students have learned to present them with their more intensive schoolwork later in the day. These needy students tend to be more receptive to an Algebra test at one o'clock as opposed to first thing in the morning. I once counseled a very explosive boy named Stephen. Most every day he came to school angry. If the teacher loaded him up with difficult work at 8:30, he would shut down. One strategy that helped was to let Stephen read, draw, or use manipulates for the first half hour or so. Eventually he would get it together and work. He couldn't be coerced.

Strategy #92

SAM'S SECRET SIGNAL

Work with your angry student to develop a secret signal that only you and he know. The student is to use the signal when he starts to get agitated. For instance, Sam has trouble dealing with criticism. He tries his best to cope with his critical peers but soon reaches a high level of frustration. He looks to Mrs. Wahlers and pulls on one of his ear lobes. She recognizes the signal and nods her head. Her nod is his permission to leave the room for a few minutes. Once Sam has calmed down, he returns to class.

Strategy #93

AFTER FIVE MINUTES IT'S LOITERING

The eighth grade team of teachers, known as the Navigators, checked their roster in August and noticed that Luis had been assigned to them. They were well aware of Luis' problems with anger, fighting, and gang membership. He was suspended six times the previous year. The teachers met to discuss Luis' behavioral plan. Did he need a structured classroom or one that was less traditional? What "crisis" plan did they need in case Luis became explosive and violent? Was he receiving counseling? Early in the school year they tried several plans to find the right fit. The following plan proved to be very successful with Luis and throughout the year his behavior improved and he was only suspended once. His anger issues were almost completely eliminated by May.

- The teachers realized that Luis needed movement. It was very difficult for him to sit very long.

- Although he needed movement, he couldn't handle it within the classroom. He tended to bother others.

- The teachers took a 12" ruler and colored it bright orange. On one side of the ruler they printed their team name, THE NAVIGATORS.

- Luis could ask permission to take the ruler and "hang out" in their hall for up to five minutes at a time as long as he didn't bother other students or classes. He had to stay on the Navigator hall so his teachers could look out and see him.

- Other teachers and principals knew that as long as Luis was carrying the orange ruler, he had permission to be in the hall.

- Whenever Luis left the room, the teacher would turn over the five-minute sand timer. Luis knew he had to return in five minutes or he would be reprimanded for "loitering." Loitering caused him to lose certain privileges.

Yes, Luis did lose some valuable classroom lessons and he did get behind a bit. But more importantly, there was great improvement with his anger control. A little freedom helped him to make progress. As his behavior improved, the other students in the class benefited because there were fewer disruptions.

Strategy #94

WHAT'S IN IT FOR ME?

Quite often angry and defiant adolescents will not back down, cooperate, or comply unless they perceive they are going to get something out of it. They present an attitude that says, "What's in it for me?" Sometimes you **may** have to let the student know "what's in it" for him or her. It may be a last resort strategy with some extremely challenging students. Following are some examples.

- **Student:** I'm not paying the stupid library five bucks for that torn book!
- **Teacher:** Garrett, did you know that many of those videos you borrow from the library are purchased with fines received from book damages and late fees?

- **Student:** I'm not giving it back!
- **Teacher:** Jessica, give it back now, then I won't have to share this incident with your volleyball coach.

- **Student:** I'm not going to the end of the line!
- **Teacher:** Mark, I'd advise to you to do it now. Don't forget, I'm considering taking some of this class back outside later today.

Strategy #95

THE CHILL FACTOR

Here is an effective tool to teach students to use when they encounter a hostile situation with another student. I've seen several versions of this, and following is the most common.

C... close mouth

H.... hands down

I... ignore

L... look for options

L... let it go

Strategy #96

STOP ARGUING AND LISTEN

Have you ever observed two teens arguing and said to yourself, "Why are they arguing? They want the same thing." Even though they seem to disagree, all teens want the same things. They want to feel liked and accepted. They don't want to be teased or left out. So why do they argue so often? The reason is they do not "really" listen to their peers. If we could teach adolescents how to be quiet and recognize the emotions of others, we could eliminate many disagreements.

Have your students read an old Sufi tale, *The Four Men and the Interpreter*, on Skill Sheet #16. Follow this activity with a class discussion.

THEY WANT THE SAME THING!

Directions: Read the following story and answer the questions. As a follow-up, share your responses with others. Start a discussion.

THE FOUR MEN AND THE INTERPRETER

Four people were given a piece of money. The first was a Persian. He said, "I'll buy with this some *angur*." The second was an Arab. He said, "No, because I want some *inab*." The third was a Turk. He said, "I do not want *inab*, I want *uzum*." The fourth was a Greek. He said, "I want *stafil*."

Because they did not know what lay behind the names of things, these four started to fight. They had information but no knowledge.

One man of wisdom present could have reconciled them all, saying: "I can fulfill the needs of all of you, with one and the same piece of money. If you honestly give me your trust, your one coin will become as four; and four at odds will become as one united."

Such a man would know that each in his own language wanted the same thing, grapes.

1. Why did the men get into a fight? _____

_____

2. How could this argument have been prevented? _____

_____

3. Can you think of a time you and your friends got into an argument only to realize later on you all wanted the same thing? Explain: _____

_____

_____

_____

_____

4. What did you learn from this old tale that was written hundreds of years ago? _____

_____

_____

_____

5. Do you agree that most teens do have similar desires, wishes, needs? _____

Strategy #97

SITTING ON THE BACK PORCH

When I look back at my childhood, I recall many positive memories. My family lived in an old farm house with a front and back porch. While sitting on the front porch my father and I would have interesting talks. We would joke and tease each other and play board games. The front porch was a safe, pleasant setting, but when dad was upset with me he would say, "Tom, we need to have a talk on the back porch." Whenever we headed out back, I knew he had some issues to discuss with me. My father believed in the importance of privacy and respect. When he had to reprimand me, I appreciated that it was done without others listening or watching.

I think that it is very important to use the "porch" theory when dealing with adolescents. If you need to confront Morris, ask him to meet with you on the back porch or some other private setting. He will appreciate you keeping the conversation out of the eyes and ears of his peers.

Strategy #98

USE THE BACK DOOR APPROACH

Many angry adolescents will sabotage all attempts to change their behaviors. In fact, some will actually say, "Don't try to change me!" Many young people believe they need their anger to survive in their dysfunctional families and violent neighborhoods. One of the worse things we can say to such a child is, "I'm going to help you with your angry problem." That statement will automatically create a barrier between you and the child. Even inviting them to an "anger management" group will get them defensive.

With my more challenging students I try not to talk about their anger during my first two or three visits. I use my "back door approach." In my early sessions with Jimmy I will play basketball with him, tell him a story (with a good moral), or play a table game. Many of my more successful sessions occur when Jimmy and I talk while playing the game Connect Four. I worked with a middle school boy named Greg that practically ran to my office every week, just so he could beat me at Connect Four. He thought the purpose of our meetings was to play table games, while I looked at our meetings as a time to sneak in some creative bits of counseling.

I worked with another young man named Gerald. He was referred to me by his mother because of his "bad attitude and temper." At the time my schedule was quite full so I had to get creative. I arranged for him to sign up for football and wrestling. From August 1 to April 1 he stayed after school every day for practice. He was very successful. I tried my best to attend some of his games and to check up on him most mornings. By the end of wrestling season his mother told me how much he improved. Could it be the sports and my support helped him with his anger more than several one hour counseling sessions? Consider using the back door approach with your more reluctant students. Help them without them realizing it!

Strategy #99

TOLERANCE TOKENS

Seldom do I ever recommend rewarding adolescents with tangible reinforcers for doing what is expected, but sometimes we may have to "prime the pump." Students often become angry because they cannot tolerate other people and/or their behaviors. When working with extremely intolerant students you may wish to use "tolerance tokens." Following is an example.

Jimmy, age fourteen, was quite prejudiced towards students in his class that were of a different race. In class he only wanted to sit near, and work in groups with others who he considered were, "Just like me." Jimmy was routinely reprimanded for make rude and racial comments. He met with a counselor who decided to use the tokens program. Jimmy's teacher was given a supply of the plastic chips. Whenever Jimmy showed signs of being tolerant of others, he was given a token. Once he earned the necessary number of tokens, he earned a special privilege.

Strategy #100

WHY ARE YOU PRAISING ME?

According to research completed by Lochman, Whidby, and Fitzgerald (2000), chronically aggressive boys often place high value on revenge behavior. For some boys, not seeking revenge is a sign of weakness, especially in front of their peers. Many have been told by parents, "Be a man and hit him back!"

Let's say you witnessed Alvin hitting Marcus. Marcus is known for his fighting and bullying, but this time he didn't retaliate; he didn't hit back. You immediately intervene and praise Marcus for his self-control. Marcus then gives you a frown as if to say, "Why are you praising me?" In his mind he doesn't deserve praise because he showed weakness by not hitting back and now many of his buddies will think less of him. Marcus has a tough guy image to uphold.

With a student like Marcus, try this. Don't praise him at that time. Stay neutral and say something like, "Marcus, come with me please." When he is not in the sight of his friends, say, "Can we talk about what just happened? Did you make a good choice?" Ease into the conversation. Hopefully he'll accept your praise in private.

Strategy #101

GIANT LEAPS

George Thompson has written an excellent book about dealing with difficult people: *Verbal Judo.* One of his first jobs involved working as a policemen in a large city. He had several scary experiences with very aggressive, violent people. He learned from these experiences and placed many of his strategies in his book. He always tried to get law breakers to comply without having to use force. He developed a five step process called LEAPS to generate voluntary compliance. I believe the LEAPS tools can help you to get upset adolescents to settle down and comply.

L **Listen.** Sincerely listen without interrupting. Look at the student and nod your head once in a while.

E **Empathy.** Show your concern. Agree that they have a right to be angry. Once the student really believes that you care, the door opens for a possible solution. If the student feels you are not sincere, the anger may increase. Thompson notes that *empathy* is possibly the most powerful word in the English language.

A **Ask.** Be creative and ask questions to help with fact-finding (who, what, when, where and how). An exchange of questions and answers often starts to calm the student.

P **Paraphrase.** Respond by saying, "Now, let me see if I've got the story correct."

S **Summarize.** Put all your thoughts and all the facts together and come up with an action plan. For instance, "I've heard both sides of the story and I've decided to think about it for awhile before I decide if any consequences are necessary."

Strategy #102

STANDING IS CONFRONTATION

If you observe adolescents in school, you'll notice that most of their bouts of arguing, teasing, bullying, gossiping, and fighting occur when they are standing. We need to do our best to encourage them to sit down with each other to discus issues/concerns. Angry levels drop immediately when people sit. When people stand, anger seldom decreases. Following is a Native American proverb that I keep posted on my office wall. I also put this proverb on colorful pens and give them to students as a reminder.

STANDING IS CONFRONTATION.
SITTING IS CONVERSATION.

Strategy #103

FLOATING THE ANGER AWAY

The Skill Sheet #17: **At the River's Edge** on the following page is a clever activity to use as a closure to an anger management program. I've used this activity with small groups and with individuals. This is a field trip, so you will need to make the necessary arrangements. This trip to the river can have a powerful and meaningful affect on your students.

AT THE RIVER'S EDGE

Objective: A field trip to help young people release their anger in a positive, memorable way. This activity is a good closure to an individual or small group counseling program.

Directions: Prior to their trip to the river have students answer these questions.

- On a separate piece of paper, list up to three things that anger you the most.
- How is your anger affecting your relationships with self and others?
- Presently, how do you deal with your anger?
- Do you believe you could do a better job controlling your anger?
- How would your life change if you could free yourself from those things that anger you?

OFF TO THE RIVER'S EDGE:

Teacher and/or counselor's instructions.

- Do the proper paper work (i.e., permission slips, transportation, etc).
- Locate a river or stream in a peaceful setting.
- Have students sit quietly at river's edge. Have them concentrate on their senses. Hear the birds. Feel the breeze. Smell the fresh air. Feel the cool water. See the sun shining.
- Once the students have relaxed for a few minutes, have them recall the three things that they said angered them the most.
- Next, they are to search for three leaves. Each leaf will represent one of their angers or triggers.
- Once they have collected their three leaves, they are to return to the river's edge.
- Tell the students, "Sometimes we have to do our best to "release" those things that anger us. We've got to let them go."
- One at a time, each student drops a leaf in the water and watches it disappear downstream. Remember, each leaf represents an anger or trigger. Encourage students to say (quietly or aloud) "I'm letting it go and won't let it anger me again." You could also have students repeat positive affirmations at this time.
- After all the leaves have disappeared, celebrate with a cheer or applause.
- Finish your visit to the river with a picnic.

Strategy #104

LET THE MUMBLERS MUMBLE

Have you ever watched a baseball game in which the batter did not agree with the umpire's call of, "Strike three!"? Instead of confronting the umpire "face-to-face," the batter walks away mumbling a few words. Sometimes we may need to be like the umpire and realize that many adolescents will not agree with our decisions. They may get angry and there may be times when our best action may be to let them mumble a few words as they walk away. As long as their comments are not extremely disrespectful, let them go. You could make the situation worse by calling them back and demanding, "What did you just say?"

Strategy #105

PUTTING THE SQUEEZE ON ANGER

Over the years I've given out hundreds of squeeze balls to students to help them control their anger. Most of the time these students take the balls to class, start tossing them around, and eventually have them taken away by teachers because the balls become a distraction. I actually had a few teachers who discouraged me from giving out stress balls. Here is an alternative to stress balls. Go to a hunting/fishing store and purchase a few floating key chains. Boaters attach keys to them so if the keys fall overboard, they won't fall to the bottom of the lake. These floating key chains have been very useful to students and teachers for several reasons. First of all, they are soft and very "squeezable." They are practically soundless. They come on a chain and the students are told to attach their floaters to a belt loop, book bag, or some other object; they are not to be removed. Some students are able to keep them in their pockets and squeeze when necessary without others noticing. Also, you can order ones that come in bright, neon colors. Students think they are "cool." You might want to consider giving one to each student in class.

Strategy #106

LET THEM DUMP THE WHOLE BUCKET

When you encounter angry students, try not to interrupt them when they are venting. Even if they are wrong, let them "dump the whole bucket." If you try to stop them and say things like, "No, Mary, that is not what happened," or "Ben, whoa! Let me say something here," the situation may get worse. Let them get it *all* out of their system before you respond. Then calmly say, "Now let me see if I understand what happened." Paraphrase what you heard and then start asking questions. Remember, whether the angry students are right or wrong, let them dump the whole bucket before you respond.

Strategy #107

A TRICKY TACTIC

Whenever you are confronted by an extremely angry or potentially violent student, you may consider utilizing a tactic known as deception. Deception is to be used when you want to surprise the student, break his/her line of intention. There are two kinds of deception.

■ **Diversion: Putting up a smokescreen……** This simply means getting the attacker off his original mission by surprising him and offering something else to look at. An example would be an eighth grade teacher saying to an angry student, "Quick, look out the window! Did you see that boy chasing that girl?" That small bit of deception or distraction may help to defuse the hostile student.

■ **Deflection: The white lie…..** Most would agree that honesty is the best policy. But, would you tell a lie to prevent getting attacked? A classroom example would be this. Mr. Hanson, biology teacher, looks at his watch as a verbally abusive student gets in his face. Mr. Hanson cleverly responds, "Oh, it's ten o'clock class. Principal Jones is supposed to be here by now. Would someone look in the hall to see if he's coming?"

Strategy #108

THE MISSING INGREDIENT IN CONFLICT RESOLUTION

I have studied numerous conflict resolution models and most of them seldom address the importance of reconciliation. According to *Webster's Dictionary*, reconciliation means, "the act of restoring friendships." Make sure that conflict resolution models in your schools mention the importance of reconciliation. Adolescents are going to argue, disagree, and even fight with their peers, but somehow they've got to learn to get along. They need to know that they can have disagreements with classmates and still remain friends.

Strategy #109

RETHINKING TRIGGERS

With some angry students it is easy to identify their triggers. Then there are some students that are difficult to understand. One day they may ignore a comment about their "big ears" and then the next day they throw a punch. Sometimes, adolescents themselves have a hard time identifying their triggers. Have your students complete Skill Sheet #18. What they learn from this activity may surprise them.

EXPLORING MY PERSONAL TRIGGERS

Directions: Anger is a normal emotion. Some people get angry quite often while others seldom do. Most anger episodes have a trigger. Triggers are happenings that can cause people to get upset. Do you know what your triggers are? Do your friends, family members, and teachers know your triggers? Take a few minutes to complete this activity. Your findings may surprise you!

■ What are my triggers? What makes me get angry?

_____

_____

_____

■ Ask your friends these questions. "What do you think my triggers are?" "What gets me angry?"

_____

_____

_____

■ Go to three teachers that know you well. Ask them to identify your triggers.

_____

_____

_____

■ Do you have brothers or sisters? Ask them, "What do you think causes me to get angry?"

_____

_____

_____

■ Ask your parents or guardians to identify your triggers.

_____

_____

_____

■ **Reflections:** What did you learn from this activity?

_____

_____

_____

Strategy #110

CHANGING THE "F" WORD TO FIDDLESTICKS

Many adolescents with anger problems have a tendency to swear. Whenever they get really combative with others, vulgarities fly from their mouths. Swearing seems to give them power and the more they do it, the angrier they get. One of the best approaches for defusing these adolescents is to focus on their cursing first, and then focus on their anger. I've noticed that if I can get them to stop swearing, their anger decreases.

Suggest a few alternate words or phrases in place of swearing. It may sound silly, but words like, "fiddlesticks" or "shucks' have helped many people. As a former child with anger problems, I used to yell out, "Jimminey Crickets!" It helped me.

Strategy #111

MIRROR THERAPY

Anger kills the face's smile and the heart's joy. Does there exist a greater enemy than one's anger?
— The Tirukural

Most adolescents are very particular about their appearance. When they get angry, they often do not look very pleasing to others. If you encourage adolescents to glance in the mirror when they are getting upset, they usually will not like what they see. An angry face can turn a pretty girl or handsome young man into an unattractive person! I remember working with a fifteen year-old girl who would pull a small pocket mirror out of her purse whenever she started to get angry. She told me that all she had to do was look at herself in the mirror and she would automatically calm down.

Strategy #112

ANGER: THE BEST FRIEND REPELLENT

When an adolescent has an anger episode in school, he or she may be losing friends without realizing it. An occasional anger outburst will not affect others much, but when Cynthia has numerous fits of anger, others may try to avoid her. Every time Cynthia inappropriately displays anger, it's like she is spraying a can of repellent at her peers. We use insect repellent to spray mosquitoes away. Many adolescents use anger as a repellent; it keeps friends away. Parents and teachers need to stress the importance of venting anger in ways that don't push potential friends away.

Have your students complete the Skill Sheet #19, **Friend Repellent**, on the following page. Then follow up with a class discussion.

FRIEND REPELLENT

Directions: Anger keeps friends away. Think of several reasons why others avoid you when you get angry.

ACME
FRIEND
REPELLENT

ANGER
guaranteed
to keep friends
away

1. _____

2. _____

3. _____

4. _____

5. _____

6. _____

7. _____

8. _____

9. _____

10. _____

Strategy #113

LET ME THINK ABOUT THAT

Whenever you get involved with a conflict between two students, you are placed in a "no win" situation. For instance, you notice Lucinda and Jasmine yelling at each other. When you intervene, you'll hear both sides of the story. Lucinda blames Jasmine and vice versa. Both want you to side with them. If you are not sure which one is the guilty party say, "Let me think about this for a while and I'll get back to the both of you soon." This may help defuse the situation temporarily. It gives the students time to cool down and it gives you time to decide what, if anything, needs to be done. I've also noticed that when I use this response, I seldom have to revisit the situation. As time passes, the students either resolve the issue on their own or they forget about it and I don't have to get involved.

Strategy #114

THEY'RE NOT TOO OLD FOR SOCIAL SKILLS GROUPS

When we think of social skills groups, we usually think of elementary school, but I have found that social skills groups can benefit middle and high school students as well. Quite often students with anger issues make more progress in groups that they do in individual counseling sessions. The reason for this is that many of their anger problems center on relationships with their peers. They need to interact with other group members, practice skills, and do some role plays. At times, students may learn more from their peers than from an adult if given a safe environment to express themselves. When you interview students with anger problems, screen each one carefully and make a decision on which arena he or she will benefit most, individual or small group.

Strategy #115

FIVE DAYS EQUALS FIVE MINUTES

One of my frequent discipline statements is, "I hate to see a student sent home for five days when he "loses" it for five minutes, or even, five seconds." So many students with anger problems get frustrated and lose control for a short period of time. They may push another student, throw a book on the floor, backtalk to a teacher, or rush out of class without permission. Then they are sent to the office. By the time they meet with the principal, they have calmed down and possibly feel remorseful, but it is too late. They get a five day suspension.

This was a dilemma I faced at my school back in 1990. I had to get creative and come up with a plan to keep these easily-angered students in school. With the help of all the staff members, we created and operated a small room called the Back-up Unit where students could go to calm down, cool off, think about their actions, and eventually return to class. The Unit is a safe environment to vent anger. The room is quiet, dull-colored, no windows, no posters on the wall, and furnished with small study carrels. Visitors are not allowed to eat in the room, do schoolwork or talk. It is to be quiet and without any stimulation. The student receives no attention, good or bad.

I have kept statistics on the room for thirteen years and I truly believe that it has helped cut down on suspension rates. To find out more about this unique program, read the book, *When All Else Fails* (www.youthlight.com).

Strategy #116

MY FAVORITE STRATEGY

Over the years I've taught students hundreds of anger management strategies. My favorite, and most effective one, is call the Pressure Point. I first wrote about it five years ago in my book, *131 Creative Strategies for Reaching Children with Anger Problems*. My personal observations have proven to me that it works most of the time. Following is the step by step procedure.

■ When a student begins to get angry, he quickly squeezes his thumb and middle finger firmly together for five to ten seconds. He may use his right or left hand. Squeeze firm enough to feel a tiny bit of pain or until it gets uncomfortable. Remember, anger is energy. By directing the angry energy into the squeezing position, it will soon diminish. Also, by pressing the thumb and middle finger together for a few seconds, it delays the student's reaction to the anger. We all know that if we can delay his response to the trigger, his outburst should not be too extreme.

■ The student is encouraged to do the Pressure Point privately by placing his hand behind his back or in his pocket. He can also place his hand under the desk.

■ Once he is settled down, he can return to work or play.

Strategy #117

FROM INJUSTICE TO CHANGING THE WORLD

Throughout history there were many well-known people who were treated unfairly. Even though there was much injustice in their lives, they fought on. Many were locked in prisons, ridiculed, beaten, and exiled. They had every right to be angry but they continued to persevere. Because of their perseverance, people like Gandhi, Martin Luther King, Jr., Rosa Parks, Nelson Mandela, and others changed the world.

Skill Sheet #20 invites students to focus on one person in history who had valid reasons to be angry, but who overcame injustice and helped make the world a better place.

THEY CHANGED THE WORLD

Directions: Throughout history many well-known people were treated unfairly. They had every right to be angry and give up. People like Martin Luther King, Jr., Rosa Parks, Gandhi, and others were arrested, put in jail, and verbally abused, but they persevered, they didn't give up their fight for justice; they changed the world. Think of a famous person who overcame injustice, anger, and bitterness. You may use one of the three mentioned here or someone else.

■ What famous person did you select? _____

■ What was this person's goal in life? What was he or she trying to change in society? _____
_____
_____
_____
_____
_____
_____
_____

■ Give some examples of how this person was treated unjustly. _____
_____
_____
_____
_____
_____
_____

■ Because of this person's perseverance, how is the world better a better place today? _____
_____
_____
_____
_____
_____
_____

Strategy #118

FROM ANGER TO BITTERNESS TO PERSEVERANCE

Rubin Hurricane Carter's story needs to be told to all adolescents. In the 1960's he was one of the top boxers in the county. In 1966 he was accused of murder and sent off to prison. He stayed there for almost twenty years when he was eventually found innocent and released. In an interview in the August 2003, *The Sun*, he talked about his anger and bitterness.

> *If I learned nothing else in prison, I learned that bitterness only consumes the vessel that contains it. I was angry for a very long time. I was eating hatred and bitterness and envy as if they were succulent morsels of buttered steak. I was angry at everything that moved. I was angry at the two state witnesses who lied. I was angry at the police who put them up to it. I was angry at the judge who allowed their testimony. I was angry at the prosecutor who sanctioned it. I was angry at the jury who accepted it. I was angry at my own lawyer for not being able to defeat it. I was furious at everyone who helped to put me in prison. (p. 6).*

Carter had every right to be angry. His anger turned to bitterness. Finally an event happened in his life that made him rethink his bitterness. In the same interview he notes:

> *One day, I was flying back from the West Coast, and in the seat pocket in front of me was a newspaper folded up to an Ann Landers column. In that column, Landers printed a poem by an anonymous author (later found to be James Patrick Kinney). I memorized that poem. The poem was called, "The Cold Within."*

Eventually he did away with his anger and bitterness and now spends most of his time helping other prisoners who have been falsely accused of crimes. Have your students read the poem, "The Cold Within." (Skill Sheet #21). Then, have a class discussion about its meaning.

THE COLD WITHIN

by James Patrick Kinney

Six men trapped by happenstance
In dark and bitter cold;
Each one possessed a stick of wood,
Or so the story's told.

Their dying fire in need of logs,
The first man held his back,
For of the faces around the fire,
He noticed one was black.

The next man looked across the way,
Saw one not of his church,
And couldn't bring himself to give
The fire his stick of birch.

The third man, dressed in tattered clothes,
Then gave his coat a hitch.
Why should his log be given up
To warm the rich.

The rich man sat back thinking of
The wealth he had in store,
And how to keep what he had earned
From going to the poor.

The black man's face bespoke revenge,
While fire passed from sight.
Saw only in his stick of wood
A way to spite the white.

The last man of this forlorn group,
Did nothing but for gain.
Give only unto those who gave
Was how he played the game.

The logs held firm in death-stilled hands
Was proof of human sin.
They died not from the cold without
But from the cold within.

Strategy #119

UNCLE JIMMIE'S PHOTOGRAPH

Several years ago I counseled a student with anger and behavior problems. The only adult in his life he trusted was an uncle named Jimmie. The boy, named Eric, always looked to him for advice. I suggested that Eric keep a picture of his uncle close by at all times. Whenever he got angry or had a tough decision to make, I told him to take out his uncle's picture, look at it, and behave in such a way that would make his uncle proud of him. Thanks to Uncle Jimmie's picture, Eric made great progress.

If you are working with a young person who is struggling, encourage him or her to carry a picture of someone he or she loves and/or respects. The student can carry the picture in a wallet, purse, notebook, or place it in a brown sleeve holder and attach to a desk. Remind the student to look at the picture when deciding how to react to anger or when making a difficult decision.

Strategy #120

DON'T COUNT NUMBERS, COUNT COLORS

Quite often angry people count to ten in an attempt stay in control of their emotions. Psychologist Leonard Felder offers a different approach. He suggests counting colors instead of numbers. For example, if Jenny begins to get angry she is to look around her environment and count at least twelve different colors. There are several reasons why this unique strategy is successful.

- It takes more of an effort than just counting to ten, giving her more time to cool off.

- It requires the individual to focus his/her attention on the task of finding twelve different colors.

- The individual eventually has to find more colors than just the basic red, white, green, yellow, and blue. He or she might have to seek out other colors such as beige, teal, orange, navy, burgundy, plum, olive, and etc.

- While Jenny is looking for different colors she will be using her fingers as a means of keeping a tally. Just the movement of fingers helps to burn off angry energy.

- Felder believes there is another reason this works. He notes that this strategy activates the areas of the brain that usually shut down when one becomes angry.

Strategy #121

THERAPEUTIC RITUALS

- A minor league baseball player always greets the home plate umpire with a hello and a smile during his first at bat of every game.

- Thirty-five year old Evelyn always parks her car at the very end of the parking lot. This allows her to get a little exercise and a taste of nature (birds singing, sun shining, etc.) before getting to her office.

- Eighth grader Lucinda gets up fifteen minutes early on school days to read her Bible and repeat a few affirmations.

- Math is very stressful to Alvin. Every time before he enters Algebra class he takes three deep breaths, taps the wall four times (four is his lucky number), and says, "I can do it!"

All of these people have problems with anger. To help them cope they practice therapeutic rituals. Each person has a series of habits or routines they utilize before entering stressful arenas. For instance, in the first example above the young baseball player had a "short fuse" and was often ejected from games for arguing with the umpire. Once he started the ritual of greeting the umpire before his first plate appearance of each game, he discovered it helped him to relate better to the umpire and eventually the two of them had fewer disagreements.

When I work with students who have anger problems, I recommend they try a few rituals to help them stay calm in stressful situations. Once the rituals become habit, progress improves. Help arm your angry adolescents with clever rituals.

Strategy #122

A VOW OF SILENCE

Many of our easily-angered students need to practice self-control. One way to do this is to have them attempt to go for a long period of time without speaking. During their times of silence they are encouraged to observe others and to truly listen. By remaining quiet they may begin to see other people's perspectives. Here are a few suggestions.

- You could rotate throughout the class so every student gets to have one day of silence.

- If you are working with an angry student, let him take a "Vow of Silence." Usually you can have the vow last one period or one day. Let other students know that he has taken a vow and to respect his silence.

- After the period of silence is over, have the student(s) write a report on their observations.

- Encourage students to implement their vows at other times. For instance, Laci may take her personal vow when she has to pass a couple rude upper grade students in the cafeteria. Henry may take a vow of silence when he is confronted by his alcoholic father. Henry realizes that at times like this his best survival skill is to remain silent.

Strategy #123

A UNIQUE WAY OF BREATHING

Here's a unique breathing strategy to share with others. It has been used for centuries in countries like China and India.

When you begin to get angry:

- Make a tube of your tongue.

- Breathe deeply through your mouth.

- Let your breathing go down into your stomach.

- Hold it for about five seconds.

- Exhale through your nose.

- Repeat at least ten times.

DEVASTATING ANGER

Strategy #124

NEVER NEVER LAND... DON'T GO THERE

It is easy to lose your cool with an angry adolescent and it is easy to get drawn in to a lengthy argument. Once this happens we need to realize that it will be us, the adults, not the children who determine how long the episode continues. Following is a list of don'ts when confronting an angry adolescent.

- **NEVER** defend your position of authority. "Because I'm the teacher and you're the student!"

- **NEVER** allow the student to get you sidetracked.

- **NEVER** cloud the issues.

- **NEVER** get too close to the student. Give him space.

- **NEVER** touch or grab. The only time to use physical restraint is when the student is hurting himself or others. I highly recommend taking a training course on restraining from the Crisis Prevention Institute.

- **NEVER** get into an argument with a student who likes to backtalk. Discipline expert Fred Jones says, "It takes one fool to backtalk, but two fools to make a conversation out of it. Backtalk is a melodrama written and produced by the student. If you take your speaking part, the show goes on. If you keep your mouth shut—the show bombs." (p. 117).

- **NEVER** compare the student to others that are well-behaved. "Look how well Luis is following class rules."

- **NEVER** dig up past histories. "Hank, you did this three times last week!"

- **NEVER** humiliate or belittle.

- **NEVER** criticize the student's peers. "You shouldn't be hanging out with Lucinda. She is always getting into trouble."

- **NEVER** use sarcasm with an explosive child. Many years ago educator and professor, A.S. Neil frowned against the use of sarcasm. He noted, "Sarcasm and humor have no connection. Humor is an affair of love, sarcasm of hate. To be sarcastic to a child is to make the child feel inferior and degraded. Only a nasty teacher or parent will ever be sarcastic." (p. 361).

- **NEVER** shout out consequences when you are angry. You may say something you will regret later.

- **NEVER** jump to conclusions. Make sure you know the whole story.

- **NEVER** try to get in the last word. It won't happen when confronting an angry adolescent.

Strategy #125

HITTING PILLOWS AND BREAKING DISHES

As recent as ten years ago many psychologists, therapists, and counselors encouraged angry people to vent their emotions by hitting pillows, punching bags, shredding paper, throwing things, or breaking sticks. These cathartic actions were believed to be helpful in assisting clients to become less angry. More recent research finds that these strategies actually make the angry person angrier. How does hitting a pillow help cure an angry person? When a girl is upset, should she use her frustration to break things? Anger gains strength by repetition. We need to help young people find less violent avenues for venting anger such as taking brisk walks, exercising, squeezing stress balls, or practicing deep breathing.

Compare the comments from two "experts" on venting anger. You decide which theory will work best in the long run in our efforts to help young people.

■ From the book, *Since Strangling Isn't an Option*, by Sandra A. Crowe:
Get a tennis racquet and hit a pillow. Work out. Break something.
I once broke all the dishes in my cabinet. It was a mess, but I
felt good. (p.97).

■ From the book, *Anger: Wisdom for Cooling the Flames*, by Thich Nhat Hanh:
A number of therapists have confirmed that the practice of venting
anger is dangerous. They told me that they stopped advising their
clients to do it. After their clients vent by hitting pillows, they are tired,
and they think they feel better. But after they rest and have some food,
if someone comes and waters the seed of anger in them, they become
even angrier than before. They have fed the roots of their anger by
rehearsing it. (p. 117).

Strategy #126

JUST WALK AWAY RENEE

You will seldom, if ever, win an argument with an adolescent. If your goal is to win such an argument, good luck! Save your energy. Don't get into a volleyball match with the student where you say something, he says something, you say something, and so on and so on. The verbal exchanges must end before things get out of hand.

With younger students you can usually tell them to return to their seat or go to time-out. They usually cooperate, but not so with middle and high school students! Sometimes the best thing to do is to excuse yourself and walk away. Say something like, "Excuse me Luke, but I need to make a phone call." You could try, "Angela, I need to go help Lenny with his math." Don't play volleyball!

Strategy #127

I DON'T APPROVE OF THAT, BUT...

Think back to when you were an adolescent. Did your parents always approve of your friends, your hair style, your clothes, and your music? Did they let you know when they didn't approve? Today's young people are not that much different than we were. We may gasp at their modern styles and music. Although we need to give them some freedom, I believe it is still important that they know our value system. In other words, when seventeen year-old Jill comes home with her hair dyed green, her father might say something like, "Jill, I don't approve of your new hair style, but I'll accept it." Here is another example. Mother walks into her seventeen year-old son's room and finds him quietly listen to a CD with vulgar language. She responds, "Son, I don't approve of that kind of music, but if you are going to listen to it, keep it in your room. I do not wish to hear it." Wearing green hair and quietly listening to a "not so nice" CD are not behaviors that most parents like, but things could be worse. With these and other "borderline" behaviors, parents may wish to implement the "I don't approve, but I'll accept" theory. Young people, although they may think we are "old fashioned," still need to know our values. If we give in to green hair and a vulgar CD once in a while, then we may have better results in dealing with these adolescents on more serious issues such smoking, drugs, alcohol, and negative peers.

Strategy #128

FLY OFF THE HANDLE

To *fly off the handle* is to lose one's composure and become uncontrollably angry. In her book, *Verbivore's Feast*, Chrysti Smith explains how the term originated.

> *The "handle" in this expression belongs to an ax whose head has detached, becoming a dangerous, hurtling missile. Early American axes were often crudely made and hafted. Sometimes Eastern manufacturers shipped only the axheads, and recipients fashioned their own handles. If the homemade handles were not crafted carefully enough to keep the head secure, the chopping blade would sooner or later part company with the handle and fly through the air with a potentially deadly mission. The pain caused by the blade descending on a nearby human target would elicit cries of anger from the victim. To "fly off the handle" sums up the rage one might feel upon being the target of a ballistic ax head.*
> (p. 126)

After reading Smith's description of the term, it made me think of something. Whenever we *fly off the handle* and get angry at something or someone, it can affect others. For instance, if Maurice gets angry at his teacher and becomes disrespectful, it causes his mother to be upset. In other words, Maurice was angry at the teacher, and his ax head flew off and struck his innocent mother. I hope this makes sense to you!

Read Smith's description of *fly off the handle* to your students. Then have them complete Skill Sheet #22. This will help students realize how their anger impacts others.

HOW MY ANGER HURTS THE INNOCENT

Directions: Ask your teacher how the term *fly off the handle* originated. After hearing the story I hope you can understand how your anger can affect innocent victims. For example, let's say you got angry at the baseball umpire and threw your bat and it hit a girl named Mandy in the crowd. You were not angry with Mandy, but she became an innocent victim of your outburst. Answer the following questions. Share your responses and thoughts with others.

■ Think of a time that you were so angry at someone that you lost your "cool" and physically hurt an innocent victim. Did you apologize? What did you learn from that event?

_____

_____

_____

_____

_____

■ Have you ever been an innocent victim of another person's rage? How did you react? Did you get angry? Did you forgive them?

_____

_____

_____

_____

_____

■ Because of your anger, did your classmates or team mates lose privileges? How did you feel when the group suffered consequences because of your actions?

_____

_____

_____

_____

■ Can you think of a time when your anger led you to say or do things wrong that caused pain or embarrassment to your parents? How did you feel about it after you settled down? Did you apologize?

_____

_____

_____

_____

Strategy #129

ON THE RADAR SCREEN

Most angry students have their outbursts in places other than the classroom. Their episodes tend to occur in various areas of the school such as the cafeteria, playground, bathrooms, and halls. Imagine that at our desks we had a small radar screen, just like the meteorologists have on television. On our radar screen we can monitor the movement of all of students. If a few of our well-behaved, trust-worthy students slipped off our screen, we wouldn't get very nervous but, if Bully Bob or Impulsive Irene can't be found, we would get very concerned. Our most violent, explosive, and aggressive students must be on our radar screens at all times. As their behaviors improve, we might let them slip off the screen once in a while.

Strategy #130

ADRENALINE IN THE BLOODSTREAM

Although it isn't always easy, do your best to remain clam when confronting a volatile student. If you remain calm, you have a better chance of calming the student. If you allow yourself to get upset, the student's behavior may worsen. Fred Jones, author of *Positive Classroom Discipline*, warns teachers:

> If you allow yourself to become upset, you will immediately affect the student in two ways, both of which are highly counterproductive. First, you will generate resentment, and it is for this resentment, compounded with public humiliation, that you will pay most dearly. Second, your upset will trigger a shot of adrenaline into the student's bloodstream just as it did into your own bloodstream. That adrenaline will not be out of either of your bloodstreams for approximately 28 minutes, and during that time the student will be hyperactive to external stimuli and will have a shortened attention span. When a teacher yells at a student, the student does not do much schoolwork for the remainder of the period. The reasons for this loss of learning time are both psychological and physiological. (p. 86).

Strategy #131

SET BACKS ARE O.K.

Have you ever been on a diet that was going well? Maybe you lost ten pounds and you were feeling proud. Then one evening while watching an old movie on television, you got a desire for chocolate ice cream. You went to the freezer to get a pint. You said to yourself, "I'll just have a couple of spoonfuls," but you ended up eating the whole pint! Did you feel guilty? Did you feel like your diet was over or did you consider the event a minor setback?

Whenever people try to change behaviors, setbacks will occur. The goal is to continue towards your goal and not to let an occasional setback get in your way. Many successful people will tell us that they learned much from their setbacks, failures, and lapses. In his book, *Making Changes Last*, the well-known therapist and author Jeffrey A. Kottler lists six positive aspects of setbacks. Share his list with adolescents who are struggling to improve their anger management skills. Let them know that setbacks happen to most people. The goal is to learn from their mistakes and move on.

WHAT FAILURES, SETBACKS AND LAPSES TEACH US:

- **Failure promotes reflection.** Kottler notes, "Without failure and relapse, people would go on about their lives without stopping to consider where they are headed and why. Failures can thus be reframed as opportunities for further growth. This is the case not only with our clients, but also in our own lives." (p.138)

- **Failure stimulates change.** When setbacks occur, successful people get creative and come up with alternatives to prevent future setbacks.

- **Failure provides feedback.** This provides an opportunity for self-talk. "What did I do wrong?" "How can I make adjustments in my program?" When setbacks happen, encourage adolescents to seek feedback from others. Friends, teachers, and family members can be very helpful.

- **Failure encourages flexibility.** Seldom do things go "according to plan." Adolescents must learn to be flexible. Creativity usually surfaces when failures occur.

- **Failure improves frustration tolerance.** Adolescents must learn how to cope with disappointments. Hopefully, after a few setbacks, they will build up a higher tolerance level.

- **Failure teaches humility.** Adolescents are often humbled when they become overconfident. A few mistakes and setbacks can be good medicine.

Strategy #132

POSITIVE CLOSURES

Try to bring positive closure to each interaction with an angry student. Even if the student completely ignores you and walks away, say something positive or encouraging. Here are a few examples.

- Things will get better. Hang in there.
- Thank you for listening.
- Tomorrow will be a better day.
- Hey, you're making progress!
- I'll touch bases with you later.

By remaining positive and optimistic, you keep the doors of communication open. Try your best to avoid these "door closers."

- Hey, you get back here right now!
- You never listen to me.
- You always think you are right!
- The next time you need help, don't come looking for me.
- When are you going to grow up?

Strategy #133

THE 'CALMER' MUST SHOW EMPATHY

Whenever you encounter an extremely angry adolescent it is crucial that you remain calm and show empathy. If you yell and get loud, it's like pouring fuel on the fire. Even a caring hand on his or her shoulder acts as a calming affect. If Jodie really believes that you care and that you are willing to listen, the odds are she'll begin to calm down. Here are a couple "do" and "do not" responses to an angry adolescent.

- **DO NOT SAY…**
  "Maureen, you stop yelling this very minute!"

  "Kenny, if you don't shut up right now I'm sending you to the office!"

  "I don't want to hear about your boyfriend problems. Stop crying and get to work!"

- **DO SAY…**
  "Maureen, settle down, honey. What's wrong?"

  "Kenny, I don't blame you for being angry. Joe should not have said that. I know your feelings were hurt."

  "Jasmine, I'm sorry about the boyfriend issue. When you settle down we can talk about it."

Strategy #134

REMOVING RUNGS ON THE LADDER OF VIOLENCE

In the book, *Angry All the Time*, the author compares the stages of anger with the rungs of a ladder. The higher one climbs the ladder, the angrier he or she gets. Parents, teachers, counselors, and other professionals must do all they can from allowing adolescents to climb too far up on their anger ladders. Utilize as many of the preventive strategies as possible that are in this book. Let's remove some of the upper rungs on their ladders. Following are the eight rungs (stages) and a brief school scenario.

- **Sneaky Anger.** John thinks his teacher is unfair. Instead of confronting her, he purposely forgets to turn in his homework and occasionally hides her pen.

- **The Cold Shoulder.** Louise is upset with Marcie. Instead of telling Marcie why she is anger, she ignores her.

- **Blaming and Shaming.** Mark seldom accepts responsibility for his actions. He likes to blame others and seems to enjoy calling them "dumb" or "stupid."

- **Swearing, Screaming, and Yelling.** When Tyra gets angry she tends to yell, scream, and curse. She may rage for several minutes before settling down.

- **Demands and Threats.** Carmen is often annoyed by Ella's teasing. Carmen threatens to "beat her up" if she doesn't stop.

- **Chasing and Holding.** Andrew accuses Sam of cheating in chess. Sam tries to leave and Andrew runs after him and restrains him against his will. Andrew threatens to hurt Sam if he cheats again.

- **Partly Controlled Violence.** Brian is accidentally elbowed in the nose while playing basketball. He turns to Alex, the boy who did it, and punches him one time in the stomach.

- **Blind Rage.** All year long Horace has been bullied and teased about being over-weight. One day he finally "loses it" and attacks Garret. He throws a chair at Garret and then follows up by punching him several times in the face. It takes two teachers to pull Horace off Garret.

*This listing is adapted from the book, *Angry All the Time*, by Ron Potter-Efron, New Harbinger Publications, 1994.

Strategy #135

APOLOGIES ARE NICE, BUT...

After students have been rude or hurtful to others, we should encourage them to apologize. Apologies are nice but not always sincere. Cheryl Jacques, head of the Washington, D.C. based Human Rights Campaign, says, "Apologies don't discourage violence, action does." Continue to encourage students to apologize but also provide them with suggestions on how they can "take action" to prove that they really are sincere. A "May I help you?" might be more effective than a "I'm sorry."

Strategy #136

FOR THOSE WHO WORK INDIVIDUALLY WITH VIOLENT STUDENTS

Counselors, psychologists, social workers, principals, nurses, and other school personnel often have to meet individually with angry and/or violent students. If you find yourself in such a situation, be prepared. See Skill Sheet #23 for a very important checklist to keep handy.

Strategy #137

DON'T FORGET FORGIVENESS

How often are the words, "I forgive you," heard in your classroom or house? I believe one of the best ways to bond with teens is to use those three powerful words when they do something wrong. You'll be amazed to find out that the more you use those words, the more the students use them. Also, it is important to know that forgiving is good for both you and the students. According to Gregg Easterbrook in his book, *The Progress Paradox*, "Research now suggests that those who take a forgiving attitude toward others not only make better friends, neighbors, and coworkers—anyone would guess that—but are themselves happier, healthier people who live longer than others and know more success in life." (p. 229)

MEETING WITH A VIOLENT STUDENT?

THE "BE PREPARED" CHECKLIST

- ☐ 1. Have a security plan in place. Alert the principals or public resource officers. Have an escape route.

- ☐ 2. On your desk keep a bell, horn, or another loud sounding device to let others know you need help immediately.

- ☐ 3. Keep squeeze balls, clay and other manipulatives on your desk.

- ☐ 4. Take an occasional deep breath to help you stay calm.

- ☐ 5. Do not let the student intimidate you.

- ☐ 6. Keep snacks, candy, gum, or soda for you and the student to share.

- ☐ 7. Always maintain a safe distance from the student.

- ☐ 8. If the violent student attempts to leave the room or run out, let him/her go. Do not attempt to stop him/her.

- ☐ 9. Do not make strong demands.

- ☐ 10. Make sure your chair is close to the door.

- ☐ 11. Do not point fingers or use threatening body language.

- ☐ 12. Do not leave potential weapons on your desk (scissors, letter openers, etc).

- ☐ 13. Learn which of your client's hands is dominant and keep to their weaker side.

- ☐ 14. Have you considered taking self-defense classes?

- ☐ 15. Do your best to end the meeting on a positive note.

*Adapted from, "Assessing Client Risk of Violence," by Lorna L. Hecker in *The Therapist's Notebook*, Hecker, Lorna and Deacon, Sharon. Hawthorne Press, NY, 1998.

Strategy #138

THE HANDY ANGER BUSTERS CHECKLIST

Make a few copies of Skill Sheet #24 for those students who are struggling with anger problems. The sheet contains fifteen anger strategies described in this book. It is designed to be cut out and placed somewhere close by so students can refer to it when they get upset. It can be glued to the inside of a notebook or taped to a desk. Some students may prefer to fold it up and keep in a purse or wallet.

Strategy #139

OFFER STUDENTS FACE-SAVING EXITS

Dr. Mel Levine, professor of pediatrics at the University of North Carolina Medical School, says, "From the moment a child gets out of bed in the morning until she is safely tucked in at night, there is a central mission: the avoidance of humiliation at all costs. We have to be careful not to subject them to public humiliation." Even with our most defiant students, we must give them face-saving exits so that they don't feel embarrassed or "backed into a corner."

There are two strategies that you can use to ensure face-saving. One way is give the defiant students choices. Another strategy involves carefully phrasing your request. Here are a couple examples:

- **Provide choices:**
  Instead of saying this to Joanie, "If you don't quiet down, I'm sending you out of here," try this, "Joanie, you need to quiet down. You can sit there and be quiet, go to the "cool down" bean bag chair, or be asked to leave. It's up to you."

- **Carefully phrase your request:**
  Instead of saying, "Barry, you better start writing now," try this, "Barry, you need to start writing now, if you don't, you may be late for football practice. The coach needs you out there today because there's a big game coming up Friday."

15 QUICK ANGER BUSTERS

Directions: Cut out this checklist and place it close by. When you start to get angry, try practicing one or two of these "anger busters."

1. **Count colors.** Instead of counting to ten, try counting colors. See if you can find at least twelve colors.

2. **Growl.** Find somewhere to be alone and let out a long, loud growl like a grizzly bear.

3. **Have a piece of gum.** Always have a piece of sugarless gum in your pocket. Then chew away your angry energy.

4. **Thought stopping.** When you start to get angry, yell to yourself, "Stop!"

5. **Go west by sailing east.** When you are angry at someone, don't take the most direct route. Take the long way. It will give you time to cool down.

6. **Chant a personal mantra.** Repeat a favorite saying several times. For instance, "Tomorrow will be a better day," or "I am a good person."

7. **Create a therapeutic ritual.** When you feel stressed and anger is on the way, use a ritual such as pulling on your right ear three times, open and close your fist five times, tap on the wall three times, snap your fingers twice, or create your own ritual.

8. **Make a vow of silence.** Promise yourself to be quiet until the anger passes.

9. **Forgive others.** When you forgive others for their actions, you'll feel better.

10. **Write in your Gratitude Journal.** When you are getting upset, write something positive in your Gratitude Journal. Think of something for which you feel thankful.

11. **Look in the mirror.** You will not like the looks of your "angry face."

12. **Are you 100% sure?** Always ask yourself this question before reacting.

13. **Try tube breathing.** Make a tube of your tongue, breathe deeply through mouth, hold for five seconds, and exhale through nose.

14. **Where's that photo?** Keep a photo of someone you love and respect. Look at the photo and ask, "How would they want me to act?"

15. **Pressure point.** Squeeze you middle finger and thumb tightly for ten seconds.

Strategy #140

EFFECTIVE CONSEQUENCING

If you have to administer a consequence to an angry student after he or she has settled down, keep these five tips in mind. They were devised by Horacio Sanchez and published in his book, *The Mentor's Guide to Promoting Resiliency*.

- The higher the individual's level of risk, the more immediate and achievable the consequence must be.

- Parties involved must reach consensus that an infraction has taken place.

- Identify the natural consequences of any behavior.

- Praise successful completion of every consequence.

- Restore normal relationships after the completion of every consequence.

Strategy #141

AFTER THE STORM: REVISITING THE 9 R'S

After your angry student has settled down, have him/her complete Skill Sheet #25. It will help the student to review what happened and it can serve as a starting point to prevent future episodes.

AFTER THE STORM:
REVISITING THE 9 R'S CHECKLIST

Directions: Think about the last event that involved you getting very angry with another person. It could have been a disagreement with a friend, sibling, parent or teacher. Write a brief description of what happened. Then go down the 9 R's checklist in order, from 1 to 9.

- With whom did you have a disagreement? _____

- What happened? _____

_____

_____

CHECKLIST

☐ 1. **Revenge.** Don't even think about it! It only makes things worse.

☐ 2. **Relax.** Sit down. Take a deep breath. Clear your mind.

☐ 3. **Regain.** Before you can resolve a problem, you must regain control of your emotions.

☐ 4. **Review.** How did the conflict start? What did you do to make things worse? Could you have walked away or asked for assistance?

☐ 5. **Reflect.** How did you feel during and after the confrontation? Were you able to effectively express your emotions? Were there witnesses to the event? How did they react?

☐ 6. **Remember.** Always remember that during a conflict, no one is 100% wrong or 100% right. Could it be that you did something wrong? Were you just as much to blame as the other person? Did you "really" listen to their side of the story?

☐ 7. **Reconciliation.** Are you able to forgive the other person? Can you forgive yourself? Were friendships restored? Did you apologize?

☐ 8. **Retool.** Now that the anger episode has passed, take time to learn new tools and strategies that will help you in the future.

☐ 9. **Retry.** Make a valid attempt to use your new tools and try to get along with those challenging people in your life.

References

Byock, Ira (2004). *The four things that matter most.* New York: Free Press.

Carr, Tom (2003). *When all else fails: 101 unique, last-resort strategies, activities and proven programs for reaching difficult students.* Chapin, SC: Youthlight, Inc.

Carr, Tom (2000). *131 creative strategies for reaching children with anger problems.* Chapin, SC: Youthlight, Inc.

Crowe, Sandra. (1997). *Since strangling isn't an option.* New York: Perigee Books.

Easterbrook, Gregg (2003). *The progress paradox.* New York: Random House.

Glasser, William (2002). *Unhappy teenagers.* New York: Harper Collins.

Hanh, Thich Nhat (2001). *Anger: wisdom for cooling the flames.* New York: Riverhead Books.

Hecker, Lorna and Deacon, Sharon (1998). *The therapist's notebook.* New York: Haworth Press.

Huler, Scott (2004). *Defining the wind.* New York: Crown Publishers.

Jones, Fred (1987). *Positive classroom discipline.* New York: McGraw Hill.

Klonsky, Ken (2003). *Changing the distance: Rubin Carter's long journey from convict to crusader. The Sun.* August.

Kottler, Jeffrey (2001). *Making changes last.* Philadelphia: Taylor and Francis.

Levine, Mel (2002). *A mind at a time.* New York: Simon and Schuster.

Lewis, Sheldon (2004). *Got bounce? Ten tips for teens to build resilience. Spirituality and Health.* August.

Lochman, J., Whidby, J., Fitzgerald, D. (2000). *Cognitive-behavioral assessment and treatment with aggressive children.* In Kendall, P. (ed.). *Child and adolescent therapy.* New York: Guilford Press.

Lochman, John and Larson, Jim (2002). *Helping schoolchildren cope with anger.* New York: Guilford Press.

Lozoff, Bo (2000). *It's a meaningful life.* New York: Viking Press.

Mackler, Carolyn (1999). *250 ways to make America better.* New York: Villard.

McGrath, Ben (2004). *Chew on. New Yorker.* February, 2.

Merton, Tom (1960). *Wisdom of the desert.* New York: New Directions.

Nay, Robert (2004). *Taking charge of anger.* New York: Guilford Press.

References
(continued)

Oppenheimer, Todd (2003). *The flickering mind.* New York: Random House.

Papolos, Demitri and Papolos, Janice (1999). *The bipolar child.* New York: Broadway Books.

Payne, Ruby (2001). *A framework for understanding poverty.* Highlands, Texas: Process, Inc.

Potter-Efron, Ron (1994). *Angry all the time.* New York: New Harbinger.

Rosen, Mark (1998). *Thank you for being such a pain.* New York: River's Press.

Sanchez, Horacio (2003). *The mentor's guide to promote resiliency.* Philadelphia: Xlibris.

Schiraldi, Glenn and Kerr, Melissa (2002). *The anger management source book.* Chicago: Contemporary Books.

Shah, Idries (1968). *The way of the sufi.* New York: Penguin Compass.

Smith, Chrysti (2004). *Verbivore's feast.* Helena, MT: Farcountry.

Thayer, Robert (2003) *The more steps the merrier. Spiritualty and Health.* December.

Thompson, George and Jenkins, Jerry (1993). *Verbal judo.* New York: Harper Collins.

West, Melissa (2000). *Exploring the labyrinth.* New York: Broadway Books.

Other Books by Tom Carr

- Keeping Love Alive in the Family

- Innovative Strategies for Unlocking Difficult Children (co-authored)

- Innovative Strategies for Unlocking Difficult Adolescents (co-authored)

- Every Child Has a Gift

- A Parent's Blueprint

- 131 Creative Strategies for Reaching Children with Anger Problems

- Monday Morning Messages

- When All Else Fails: 101 Unique, Last-Resort Strategies, Activities, & Proven Programs for Reaching Difficult Students

- Return to the Land: The Search for Compassion